Planning for People

Essays on the Social Context of Planning

Maurice Broady
Senior Lecturer in Sociology
University of Southampton

The Bedford Square Press
of The National Council of Social Service
26 Bedford Square   London   WC1

© Copyright NCSS 1968
NCSS Reference number 765
SBN 7199 0765 9

The views expressed in these essays are those of the author,
and not necessarily of the National Council of Social Service

Printed in England by Latimer Trend & Co Ltd Plymouth

Contents

Introduction

The publication of this book was sparked off by a request from the National Council of Social Service for permission to publish 'The Idea of Social Planning' as an occasional paper. Though I was quite ready to agree to this request, one or two considerations led me to think that the time was ripe to publish a collection of essays on this general theme. For one thing, it was a nuisance to have to have photo-copies made to meet requests for offprints of articles, and my students also found it inconvenient to have to search out the many recondite journals in which they had originally appeared. But there was a more substantial reason. This particular paper on social planning had been given at the Royal Society of Health Congress in 1967. It had been invited at the suggestion of a county planning officer and it was to be published in the journal of his profession. And yet it spoke equally to the concerns of the National Council of Social Service. I was particularly pleased about this. For this paper, like the others in this series, had grown out of my own twofold interest, as an applied sociologist, in urban planning and the role of voluntary associations in a democratic society; and it was encouraging to find that it spoke equally to people concerned with both these issues.

Yet it was clear that many of the practitioners in these fields did not understand how these issues might interlock – or even suspect that they did so. The XIII International Conference of Social Work, for instance, which was held in Washington in 1966, was concerned with urban development and its implications for social welfare, but the British delegation included only one town planner. A year ago, the National Institute for Social Work Training convened a one-day meeting to discuss Marris and Rein's study of social reform in American cities: and again the audience consisted almost exclusively of social workers of one kind or another. By the same token, the requests for offprints, which had come mainly from architects and planners, showed that they were taking up one side of my thinking without appreciating that it was interlocked with arguments, published elsewhere, about social organisation; and it seemed likely that social workers were also seeing only one side of what for me were two interrelated parts of the same theory.

Certainly, there is evidence of a growing interest in the way in which the physical planning and social organisation of urban areas should be co-ordinated. Sir Hugh Wilson, best known perhaps as the chief planner of Cumbernauld New Town, spoke in this idiom to the Washington Conference. More recently, Wilfred Burns, in his presidential address to the Town Planning Institute, made a plea for town planning and social planning to 'go hand in hand with common objectives and constant interchange of views on problems and ideas'. Much the same concern informs the report on *The Needs of New Communities* which the Central Housing Advisory Committee published in 1967. Yet, at the moment in Britain, as compared with the United States, the idea that some kind of social planning needs to be integrated with land-use and economic planning is only just beginning to struggle towards acceptance, and that very tentatively and pragmatically. My main purpose in publishing these papers as a collection, therefore, is to make some contribution to this embryonic development.

In my view, the academic's most useful contribution to affairs is to reflect upon the theoretical implications of what is done in practice. A distinction must constantly be made between institutions which have primarily an executive role and those whose function is primarily reflective. An industrial firm or a government department are of the one kind, a university of the other. To make this distinction is in no way to scorn practice, still less to subscribe to that fallacious view, so characteristic of English empiricism, that theory and practice are radically separate from each other. For all practice invokes theory and major theoretical issues are inevitably raised by engaging in, and then reflecting upon practical affairs. In a very real sense, the *éminence grise* of this book is John Mack, now director of the School of Social Study at Glasgow University, for it was in a most stimulating period of collaboration with him, some ten years ago, that many of the seeds were sown which have ripened into these papers. On one occasion when I was preparing an address for a conference of housing managers, Mack expressed his view of an academic's function in the following way: 'Take them theory, Broady, (he said) take them theory: if *you* don't take it them, nobody else will – and that's *your* job.' It is in that spirit that these papers were written.

That there are a number of fairly coherent themes running through these essays will, I hope, be evident to the reader. But since they were written independently of each other, for particular purposes and with particular audiences in mind, it may be helpful to explain briefly what line of argument links them together. This will also help to make my reason clear for placing them in the order – rather different from that in which they were written – in which they now stand.

The argument runs roughly as follows. Town planners, and particularly architect-planners, have tended to be social idealists. They have been heir to a tradition of utopian thinking which has led them to envisage the creation of ideal communities for people to live in. The professional tools at their disposal have been the tools of architectural design and it is understandable that they should have come to believe that desirable social aims can be secured by the effective design of the physical environment. The social theory which is written into this outlook – which I have tried to illustrate and criticise in 'Social Theory in Architectural Design' – is what I have called 'architectural determinism': the simple idea that a good physical environment will necessarily produce good social effects.

Now in my view, this theory vastly overstates the importance of physical design for the achievement of social goals. However, if negative criticism is to avoid the charge of being merely destructive, it must be followed up by an attempt to spell out a more viable theory on which practice can be based. Most of the other papers, I trust, have something more obviously positive to say. Essentially, the point which I am making is that the achievement of social objectives in the planning of urban areas – of neighbourliness, to take a trite example – must take account not only of physical design but also of the people who are involved and of the patterns of social organisation, and particularly of administration, that are set up in those areas. It has been shown, for example, that the kind of work produced in architects' offices is systematically related to the way in which those offices are organised. This kind of understanding has been developed in what sociologists call organisation theory; and in 'Social Theory and the Total Environment', I suggest that the extension of this kind of theorising to urban problems would lead us to expect different patterns of urban organisation to have very different effects upon what might be called the social output of urban areas.

The third paper 'Community Power and Voluntary Initiative' explores this point in one particular context. It argues that our system of government and the political assumptions which it embodies may restrict, even if they do not entirely stifle, the contribution which voluntary associations may make within a community. Yet, as the following paper on 'Social Change and Town Development' notes, the scale of voluntary enterprise is growing in the Welfare State, though its orientation has been changing, as the social changes that are brought about by modern technological developments produce within the community an increasingly well-educated and socially active population: and that this is something to which our planning system is already beginning to adjust and to which the whole pattern of social administration will have to attune itself before this century is through. The nub of the fifth paper on 'The Idea of Social Planning' is that we shall have to move, in our thinking on these matters, well beyond the conventional ideas on social planning which have thought of its function as being to provide the physical fabric to meet specific social needs, to seeing that it also has to do with finding how to incorporate the social potential of a community within the planned development of urban regions.

Some of the impetus which underlies this kind of thinking came from preparing a report on 'The Social Aspects of a Town Development Scheme', which was commissioned by the Basingstoke Town Development Joint Committee in 1963. Inevitably, the format of this report (which appears here as Chapter 6) is rather different from that of the other essays which were originally drafted as contributions to conferences of one kind or another. But it has been included in this collection because it indicates the kind of practical implications which follow from the approach which is elaborated in the other essays and because it was in this report that I first spelled out the different kinds of contribution which physical design, the people themselves (regarded as having not only problems but also potentialities) and social organisation could make to the achievement of social goals.

The final paper 'The Social Context of Urban Planning' was prepared for the Alcan universities conference on planning in September 1967. The last to have been written, it rounds off the argument of this book by developing these ideas a little more in depth and also by considering what positive contribution the sociologist can make to problems of urban planning. Its main point in that regard is that the sociologist is likely to be the more effective if sociology is thought of not simply as a matter of empirical fact-finding, of 'doing a survey' but rather as a matter of theoretically-based argument. Attending to the theory of planning, however, inevitably raises the question of how far it is possible to plan at all, in conditions of very rapid social change. In my opinion, one must accept a high degree of indeterminacy in human affairs and this sets constraints upon the possibilities of prediction and thus of determinate planning, notwithstanding the great advances that are presently being made in planning technology.

The central question therefore is: how can the necessity for planning be accommodated to an awareness of social indeterminacy? From a positivist standpoint, which regards society and man, in principle at least, as subject to the same kind of laws as natural phenomena and which is confident that a knowledge of social scientific laws will make possible a completely rational form of social planning: from this point of view, to acknowledge indeterminacy is to admit defeat, for it is supposed that determinate control and prediction waits only upon the development of more precise techniques of investigation. But if indeterminacy is regarded as inherent in human existence, then a rather different kind of planning theory has to be worked out. In such a theory the role of social initiative – unpredictable both in its inception and its outcome – becomes a crucial element in the progress of society; and the development of potentialities within a society, though they cannot be precisely predicted, becomes something which planning must actively seek to foster and encourage. Planning, accordingly, has to be thought of not only as a matter of physical design and economic policy but also as a social process of an educational kind which seeks to encourage the contributions which people themselves can make to the improvement of their own social environment.

In the last few years, some moves in this direction have begun to be made. The interest which planners have recently been showing in citizen participation; the incorporation into the Town and Country Planning Bill, which is at present going through Parliament, of proposals designed to give the citizen a greater opportunity for discussing plans while they are still at a formative stage; the growing interest in American thinking which regards social planning as closely related to physical and economic planning: these are indications of changes that are slowly taking place in the climate of opinion in Britain. But there is still work to be done. And what now needs to be worked out is a more viable theory of social planning which could provide a sounder basis for practice than we presently have at our disposal.

These essays are best regarded as an approach to such a theory. They are intended to provoke thinking; they can claim no more than that. As all bar one of them have already been published elsewhere, I wish to thank the various editors who have allowed me to reprint them in this volume. Since this edition is intended for a wide and non-specialist readership, the weighty apparatus of scholarly footnotes, which in one article alone ran to well over sixty, has been jettisoned. If the reader should wish to follow up references, he can trace them by referring to the appendix where the journals in which they first appeared are noted.

It is inevitable that there should be some repetition in a collection of essays of this kind. That this has been cut to a minimum is due entirely to the excellent job of editing the original manuscripts which was undertaken with so sensitive a pen by Mr. J. W. A. Thorburn, to whom I express my warmest appreciation. I also wish to thank Mrs. Lottie Nixon for preparing the original typescript with such care, and Mr. Gerald King and his staff in the Publications Department of the National Council of Social Service from whose concern for quality this volume (and I myself) have greatly benefited. Finally, in a publication like this – as compared with the solemn columns of learned or would-be learned journals – it is possible to give rein to one's conviction that genuine seriousness of purpose is not inconsistent with a touch of humour. I am therefore delighted that David Austin should have put me still further in his debt by contributing to this volume such an excellent set of cartoons.

MAURICE BROADY
Southampton April 1968

Social Theory
in Architectural
Design

One does not have to talk with architects and town planners for very long to discover that they are interested in social theory. There are, of course, the aesthetes pure and simple – the people I used to meet in the Liverpool School in the early fifties, whose fifth-year schemes were likely to be designs of swish villas for equally swish colleagues on the Riviera. But most of the designers I meet now, especially at the Architectural Association, are better described as 'social consciences'. They are idealists – even radicals. They share a sense of social purpose. They want to improve society and they believe that their work as architects or planners can help them to do so. They are, accordingly, interested in sociology. They have read their Geddes and their Mumford and now know all about the mums of Bethnal Green and the sidewalks in Greenwich Village. They talk a lot about 'survey before plan'; they have even consorted (not perhaps very profitably) with the odd sociologist like myself.

For my part, I greatly enjoy these encounters with people who are convinced of the importance of their work and bubbling over with the desire to create new and better environments. It is a change from the atmosphere of a university where creativity may often be inhibited and vision narrowed by the demands of scholarship. I would not wish in any way to weaken this ardour and idealism. And yet, at times, one stands aghast at the naivety, the sheer lack of intellectual discipline which often marks the enthusiastic designer's confrontation with social theory. Perhaps one ought not to worry about all this hot air: for it may not be taken seriously even by its exponents. Indeed, it sometimes seems to be used not so much to guide design as to bolster morale and to add a patina of words to ideas intuitively conceived. In the end, however, one *must* be concerned. For phoney social theory is likely to produce phoney expectations and spurious designs. It may equally hinder effective collaboration between social scientists and designers and inhibit the development of more valid ideas about the relationship between architectural design and social structure. That is why a largely critical article (which this will be) is not as negative as might at first be supposed. For one of the best ways to begin to elaborate new ideas is to criticise the inadequacies of current theory.

At least three types of architectural theorising can be found. There is, first of all, straight waffle: 'The vertical segregation of traffic as *an urban system* (meaning?) offers us potentially one effective component (why effective if only potentially offered?) in such a *shaping-strategy* (what?) not simply because *in organisational terms* (meaning again?) for example, cars can get to the right place without even having to cross pedestrian lines on the same plane, but because the very independence of each layer offers *a potential for generating a new urban syntax* (coo!) in as much as it allows for independent development of each level, etc.' I suppose this simply means that the vertical segregation of traffic and pedestrians enables cars to move without bumping into people and allows traffic and pedestrian areas to be developed independently of each other: which is a good deal less significant a point than the original form of expression would lead one to imagine.

The second type of theorising involves grafting a spurious social theory on to a useful and sensible technical solution. This is evident in a review of Denys Lasdun's cluster-blocks in Bethnal Green which states: 'The cluster concept offers a viable alternative on the visual side by creating tower accents without visually destroying the existing grain; on the human side it shows promise in possessing domestic scale in the component parts of those towers and maintaining something like the pre-existing sociological groupings of the street that gave the original urban grain to the district.' To which one sociologist has tartly commented that 'the sociological thinking has been grafted on to an aesthetic dogma, and it has been assumed, without observation, that the graft has taken successfully and is bearing fruit. It might have been less confusing simply to explain that if housing policy required sixty-four households to be accommodated on such a small site then they would have to live in some form of high tower or slab, in which case a cluster block would look better than anything else.'

I myself first came across this unnecessary grafting of social ideas a number of years ago when a well-known architect was explaining the principle of vertical segregation of pedestrians and traffic. He had made an extremely good technical case for this idea; and he concluded – in no flippant manner – by arguing, on completely redundant social grounds, that this design would be entirely consonant with the *Zeit-geist* of the second half of the century (or something) since it would enable pedestrians to enjoy the sight of myriads of brightly-coloured cars flashing along below them and thus to be more fully part of the exciting flux of an automobile era. The *exact* detail of expression may well have escaped me in this example: but no-one who has heard enthusiastic architects in their romantic vein will doubt its plausibility. Nor can one doubt that the function of these various kinds of utterance is not so much to clarify social understanding as to cheer their authors up and to show what remarkable chaps they really are. This kind of thinking may be necessary for the designer's morale and thus have *something* useful to contribute to his profession. But it is much more likely to confuse understanding and jeopardise clear thinking.

Architectural determinism

Architects, however, are apt to subscribe to a much more fundamental and pervasive kind of theorising which may be labelled 'architectural determinism'. It is more often found implicit in architects' thinking than in any clearly argued form: and it is probably the more dangerous for that. How influential it is, is difficult to say. But the fact that it has been vigorously defended in at least four architectural schools in which I have had occasion to criticize it and that it has also been the subject of critical comment by other sociologists on both sides of the Atlantic supports the view that it is fairly widely held among architects and town planners. Nor is it difficult to catch examples. There was, for instance, the group-architect at Cumbernauld who asked my advice on whether it would be socially more desirable to place three point-blocks in triangle rather than in line. Then there was the planner at Basingstoke who assured me that the most satisfied and well-settled residents in the four estates which we were studying in the town would be found in the one that was outstanding in layout and design. Quite the reverse was in fact the case – 24 per cent of the residents of that estate expressed themselves dissatisfied as compared with only 11 per cent in the three other estates. And the Cumbernauld architect was rather taken aback when I said that I doubted whether it would make any real difference socially which way he placed his point-blocks!

That these expectations were both wrong is less interesting than the fact that they were held. For they indicate very clearly the assumptions which derive an implicitly-held theory of architectural determinism. The theory has been expressed as follows: 'The architect who builds a house or designs a site plan, who decides where the roads will and will not go, and who decides which directions the houses will face and how close together they will be, also is, to a large extent, deciding the pattern of social life among the people who will live in these houses.' It asserts that architectural design has a direct and determinate effect on the way people behave. It implies a one-way process in which the physical environment is the independent, and human behaviour the dependent variable. It suggests that those human beings for whom architects and planners create their designs are simply moulded by the environment which is provided for them. It is of a kind with the other varieties of popular determinism – such as the view that national character is determined by climate – which save the layman the trouble and worry of observing accurately and thinking clearly.

The neighbourhood unit theory

The classic case of architectural determinism is the neighbourhood unit theory. Here again, a dubious social theory was grafted on to a reasonable technical solution. The neighbourhood unit idea, as it was first elaborated by Clarence Perry in the nineteen-twenties, was essentially a means of relating physical amenities systematically to population, with particular regard to the safety and convenience of pedestrians and especially children. Certainly, Perry's *social* claims for the neighbourhood unit were very careful and extremely modest. Much the same could be said of the Dudley Report in which the idea received semi-official endorsement when it was published in 1944; while the report prepared in 1943 by the National Council of Social Service on *The Size and Social Structure of a Town* similarly argued that 'Though physical planning and administrative measures *cannot by themselves change social relationships,* they can, if wisely and positively conceived, encourage and facilitate the growth of that spirit of fellowship without which true community life is impossible.' As so often happens, however, the qualifications embodied in this statement were in practice largely ignored. To the theory of how to allocate amenities in housing areas, which the nieghbourhood unit idea originally was, there was added after the war a crude social theory which asserted that the neighbourhood plan, and the way in which amenities were allocated within it, *would* foster a sense of belonging and community spirit among the residents of each neighbourhood.

One of the major puzzles in the history of recent planning theory is why this idea should have been so enthusiastically received in the years immediately after the war. (Why, indeed, despite all the criticism to which it has been subjected, does it still find such ardent defenders not only in this country but in the United States and on the Continent, too?) I think the answer is that it was really ideological; that it was accepted not because it could be shown to be valid, but because it was *hoped* that it would be so. You have only to think of the circumstances in which it was accepted to appreciate why this should have been the case. The new town idea had been buttressed by the criticisms which had been levelled at the inter-war housing estates. These estates had been criticised not only because they were ugly, badly-designed and lacking even the basic social amenities, but also because the people who lived in them were said to miss the friendliness, neighbourliness and the sense of belonging to a definite community which, despite bad housing and a poor physical environment, they had enjoyed in the slum districts from which they had been moved. How then, could the good housing of the new estates be combined with the friendliness of the slums? That was the sort of problem with which socially-conscious, idealistic planners, architects, social workers and administrators were concerned in the nineteen-thirties.

In the answer which they found, the assumptions of architectural determinism stand out clearly. What was it about the slum street that made it so friendly? Obviously, they said, its amenities: its pubs and church halls and, above all, the dear little corner shops where Ma could get 'tick' to bide her over till wage night and meet her friends for a chat. The answer for the new towns, then, was to provide the same kind of amenities (especially the little corner shops) and *eureka!* people would be as friendly and neighbourly in their new surroundings as they had been in the old. Of course, people do meet each other and chat in pubs and corner shops. But not all pubs and corner shops engender the neighbourliness of the slum street. Of much more importance in explaining neighbourliness are the *social* facts, first, that the people who lived in the slums had often lived in the same street for several generations and thus had long-standing contacts with their neighbours and kin; and second, that people who suffer economic hardship are prone to band together for mutual help and protection. It is true that neighbourliness is induced by environmental factors. Of these, however, the most relevant are social and economic rather than physical. But it can be readily understood why planners (and others who wished to do something to make life better for their fellow-men) should have been so ready to suppose that the prime factor in the growth of 'community spirit' was the design of the *physical* environment which it was uniquely in their power to modify.

Inadequacies of current theory

There is no reason to expect that idealistic young architects graduating now will think any differently. The disposition which I am criticising has its roots deep in the intellectual bias of the architectural profession. We are all inclined to see the whole world through our own professional spectacles, and thus to see it distortedly. The lawyer, dealing daily as he is with divorces and separations, often seems to suppose that the family is held together only by the constraint of the law. Once admit a modification of the divorce laws, he seems to be saying, and fornication will be rampant and we shall all be running off with our neighbours' wives. The physicist is apt to suppose that the world could be run much better if only scientists were in charge; the psychologist, that the assumptions about rat behaviour that are helpful in the lab are equally valid as general principles of human conduct. By the same token, the designer may easily come to believe that his work will achieve the social objectives which not only his client, but he himself, wishes to promote.

Nor does the architect's training help him to understand, except in a very superficial way, the approach of the social scientist to the kind of problems he is interested in. Sociologists, it is true, are invited to give short courses of lectures in many architectural schools. But they are usually expected to contribute on such a narrow, vocationally-oriented tack that it is difficult for them to communicate so that it sinks in what social theory is all about, how it is established and by what criteria it should be evaluated. Architectural students, therefore, tend to get a general notion of how social surveys are conducted but – even if they are told – they usually fail to appreciate that a survey forms only part of a sociological argument and that it is in order to provide particular kinds of evidence for such arguments that surveys are undertaken. In my opinion, it is this imbalance between a rigorous training in visual and a superficial training in social scientific thinking that makes it possible for architectural students to accept a deterministic answer to the complex problem of how social organisation and architectural design interact; and which thus contributes to that extreme, at times even obsessive anxiety about the effects that their work is likely to have on other people's lives which one so often notices in them. A further result of this imbalance, which has been noticeable on every 'jury' I have ever attended at the Architectural Association school, is that students tend to collect lots of factual information only to be at a loss what to do with it all once they have got it, and frequently fail to control their intuitive designer's approach with coherent and systematic thinking.

The superficiality of architects' social theory can be shown quite as clearly in the detail of planning practice. In one planning scheme in which I was recently involved, the problem was being considered how shops should be allocated in residential areas. Two divergent views were advanced. On the one hand, it was proposed that, in order to maximise convenience, suites of shops should be located so that no resident was more than a quarter of a mile from one of them. This would have meant building one suite of 6,000 square feet for every 3,000 people. The alternative view held that the overriding criterion in allocating shops was 'to establish focal points that will foster a sense of community within the area served'; and this, it was argued, would be more effectively achieved by building one suite of 9,000 square feet for every 5,000 people.

This second view is a typical expression of the neighbourhood unit idea that amenities should be sited so as to foster a sense of community. But the idea that such a minor difference of size as that between 3,000 and 5,000 people would have any material influence upon something so nebulous as a sense of community is sheer speculation masquerading as sociological truth. Neither figure can be said to be more valid than the other in this connection. Furthermore, even if differences *could* be shown in the degree of community feeling in neighbourhoods of different sizes, it would still remain open to doubt whether such differences were caused, or even directly influenced by the size of the neighbourhoods or the way in which amenities were disposed within them. Accordingly, this kind of 'sociological' argument seems designed to support a proposition which, if it were valid, would be so for reasons quite different from this.

At first glance, the convenience argument seems much more plausible. It does not depend upon the singularly narrow definition of social welfare that is involved in regarding the development of community feeling as the primary criterion in allocating shops, and it at least seeks to achieve some tangible benefit for the consumer. Yet it is curious how narrow and conventional was the designer's view of what benefits the consumer might wish to have maximised. Convenience, after all, is only one aspect of economy: it is a measure of the economy of time and distance. But there is also economy of the purse. The housewife surely wants shops that are both convenient and cheap; and if the convenience of having shops within a $\frac{1}{4}$ mile of everybody meant that only one grocer could make a living in each suite of shops, this might encourage, even if it did not oblige him to charge monopoly prices which could probably be avoided if convenience were marginally reduced, by increasing the radius served by the shops, in order to have two grocer's shops in competition with each other. Thus, the fact that the planner was thinking primary in terms of *physical* distance prevented him from thinking realistically about shopping provision by taking into account all the social requirements which shops need to meet. In such simple but significant ways does inadequate social theory hinder sound thinking about design problems.

The counter-argument

But to return to the basic issue of the effect of architectural design on social organisation. Surely, it will be argued, buildings and lay-out *do* influence social behaviour? There is certainly some evidence to support this view. In the end, one is likely to develop social contacts with people one meets, and whom one meets within a residential area *is* affected by its lay-out. A number of studies of planned communities both here and in America have certainly shown the significance of proximity in the formation of social relationships. Their conclusions have been summed up in the phrase: 'People select their friends primarily from those who live near by and those whom their house faces.' Even the location of a kitchen door can matter! If it is at the side of the house, contacts are more likely to be made with the side-neighbour; if at the back of the house, with the party neighbour.

These data, however, valid though they are, have been used to support the belief that 'the tenants' entire social life may hang on the smallest whim of the greenest draftsman . . .'. But this kind of conclusion is hardly justified. In the first place, the relationship between proximity and friendship is obviously not absolute, for friendships *are* made with people who live down the street as well as in adjacent houses and in districts far away as well as near at hand. Even though Leo Kuper's study of a Coventry estate showed that more intensive interaction between neighbours took place in cul-de-sacs than in long terraces of houses, there is also evidence that, in older areas of terraced-housing, street groups may be even more cohesive and active. The second point is that, while design features may facilitate neighbourly intercourse, they cannot be said to influence its quality. Those who subscribe to architectural determinism always seem to suppose that the influence of design will be beneficial. But people may be rancorous as well as friendly, and, as several studies of neighbouring families have shown, they may equally well wish to defend themselves against their neighbours as to welcome every opportunity to meet them. How they will react to their physical environment depends on so much more than physical design; and if propinquity provides the occasion for contact between neighbours, how that contact develops depends chiefly upon social factors.

The Basingstoke example which was quoted earlier illustrates the point very clearly. The reason why the residents of the best-designed estate were the least satisfied was that their satisfaction depended only marginally upon architectural design. Broadly speaking, the working-class residents of the other estates had moved in order to get better housing. They, therefore, were well satisfied to have a house of their own, away from nagging in-laws and rapacious London landlords. The middle-class residents of the well-designed estate, on the other hand, had mostly had a decent enough house before moving to Basingstoke and had moved chiefly to get a better job. For them, the fact that they were living in a reasonably well-designed house in the best laid-out estate in the town was inadequate compensation for their general disappointment with the social life of Basingstoke itself.

Two other examples will suffice to clinch the point. In one university a few years ago, the attempt was made to encourage staff and students to meet together informally by installing a coffee-lounge between the senior and junior common rooms, especially furnished with comfortable chairs and thick carpets. This did not work. Nor, without supporting social and possibly administrative arrangements, could it possibly have done so. For it is quite unrealistic to suppose that the provision of a coffee-lounge could change a pattern of social segregation which rests upon substantial differences of function and responsibility, not to mention age and status, and which the whole pattern of academic organisation tends to emphasise.

Conversely, social intercourse, if deeply enough rooted, may continue in the teeth of architectural disincentives. The Institute of Community Studies, for instance, in a study of tenant reaction to four contrasting types of housing in the East End of London, found that the people who felt most cut off from their neighbours and who considered that the layout of the building made it particularly difficult to keep in touch with other tenants, were the residents of Denys Lasdun's cluster-block, but that these same tenants were nevertheless much more sociable than the residents of the other types of building. The reason had to do with their social background. For most of them had previously lived in one of the most gregarious tenements in the district and they simply carried on these social activities, such as baby-sitting for one another, visiting and going shopping together, which over time had become part of their way of life.

In the light of such evidence, therefore, even if it be admitted that architectural design may influence, it cannot be said to determine social behaviour. Indeed, there is much to be said for the view that it has, at most, only a marginal effect on social activity. Among other evidence, it is particularly interesting to note that whenever architects are discussing their own domestic affairs this is the view which they invariably appear to adopt. In the recent discussions that have been going on about the future of the Architectural Association school, it was, I suggest significant that the discussion was much less concerned with the present fabric and its many inadequacies than with the constitution of the school in these new circumstances – with how it should be organised as a *social* institution. By the same token, the RIBA report on *The Architect and his Office* was equally unconcerned with the physical aspects of architectural offices but focused again upon the way in which those offices were organized. If architects pay so little attention to architecture when their own professional activities are at issue, it is surely odd that they should be so excessively concerned with it when *other* people's affairs are concerned and so persuaded that architectural design can have the great effect upon them which they are inclined to ignore for themselves!

Towards a more viable social theory

Clearly, then, as social theory, architectural determinism will not do. So where do we go from here? The answer is that we must now begin to develop a more realistic understanding of the relations between architectural design and human behaviour: one, that is to say, which reflects what actually happens rather than what we hope might happen. I say 'begin' advisedly, because in this country at least, we have barely started to consider the problem systematically. All I can do here, therefore, is to make some very general remarks about some of the considerations that need to be taken into account.

These days, architects and planners are concerned not simply with buildings but with environments. As Sir Hugh Wilson has put it: 'If it (planning) is concerned *with the total environment*, with the creation of towns of quality and character *and with the well-being of people*, then I claim to be a planner.' The assumption which I have been criticising is that environment is created uniquely by buildings and physical design. The first step in correcting this theory is to introduce the useful distinction, put forward by the American sociologist Herbert Gans, between a potential and an effective environment. The point of this distinction is clear enough. The physical form is only a potential environment since it simply provides possibilities or cues for social behaviour. The effective – or total – environment is the product of those physical patterns plus the behaviour of the people who use them, and that will vary according to their social background and their way of life: to what sociologists, in their technical language, call social structure and culture.

This distinction entails two simple but important points which now need to be made clear. Designers often fail to realize how much difference it makes to their view of the world that they respond to buildings and townscapes with eyes more discriminating and intellects more sensitive to design than those of the average layman. Their failure to appreciate the point leads them to make the fallacious assumption that the users of buildings will react to them as they do themselves. There is substantial evidence to justify our being very sceptical of this belief. One inquiry, for example, found that tenants in a Scottish housing estate noticed and complained about practical things, such as the lack of made-up footpaths, but failed to remark upon the unsightly colliery slag-heaps or the monotonous appearance of their houses. Indeed, in another estate, they even failed to distinguish between an older and a more modern style of housing. A similar conclusion came out of a study of a Glasgow redevelopment scheme in which the authors were surprised to find how comparatively insensitive the tenants were to questions of design. Nearer home, reactions to the Smithsons' 'Economist' building ranged from the sophisticated comments of architects to the negative responses of members of *The Economist* staff, of whom one critic reported that he 'asked several of our people but failed to get an answer to the question: Does this place stimulate or not?'.

A similar disparity must also be noted between common-sense assumptions about the way human beings react to environmental stimuli and how they actually do react. The psychology of design is singularly ill-developed; but what we *do* know about it suggests that we should be equally cautious about common-sense, layman's psychology. For example, it has always been assumed that people can judge accurately how much daylight there actually is in a room. An investigation by Brian Wells of the Department of Building Science at Liverpool University, however, has shown that 'the strength of beliefs about daylighting and view were *independent of physical context* . . . and that people tended to overestimate the proportion of daylight that they had to work by at increasing distances from the windows.' Any theory of the relationship between design and human behaviour, therefore, needs to take full account of the empirical evidence adduced by social scientists which calls common-sense ideas so clearly in question.

The second point which we must go on to make is that human beings are a good deal more autonomous and adaptable than a deterministic theory would lead one to suppose. Architects, indeed, especially those who use prefabricated and standardised dwellings, have been criticised for 'stamping people to a common mould'. The answer to this sort of criticism is simply to go and look at the interiors of those standardised rooms – better still, at the interior designs of the even more standardised cupboards in army barrack-rooms – to appreciate how little individuality is inhibited by standardisation.

Furthermore, people may well be more adjustable than is often supposed. A study of the Worsley overspill estate, for instance, found that, although 54 per cent of the residents had not wished to leave Salford, by the time they had lived in Worsley for a few years, only 17 per cent of them wished to return to the city. Similarly, while any movement of population inevitably causes some personal disturbance which people dislike, all the evidence shows that, for most people, this is a temporary phase and that they settle equally well in the new area as in the old.

A further demonstration of the point came from an inquiry into the tenants' reaction to moving into the first precinct of the Hutchesontown-Gorbals redevelopment scheme in Glasgow. The scheme comprised flats and maisonettes. Allocation to the houses was made by ballot, so that it was a matter of chance which kind of dwelling each tenant got. When the tenants were asked about their preferences, it was discovered that the flat-dwellers preferred the flats and the maisonette-dwellers the maisonettes and that each group of tenants justified its preference by criticising aspects of the other type of dwelling which did not trouble the people who actually lived in them.

Conclusions

Two main conclusions follow from all this. First, architectural design, like music to a film, is complementary to human activity; it does not shape it. Architecture, therefore, has no kind of magic by which men can be redeemed or society transformed. Its prime social function is to facilitate people's doing what they wish, or are obliged to do. The architect achieves this by designing a physical structure that is able to meet known and predictable activities as conveniently and economically as possible. However, human behaviour is like runny jelly – not formless, but wobbly and changeable; and since he cannot predict its changes, the designer also has to allow as best he can for such new demands as may come to be made on his buildings. More positively, perhaps, it is open to to him to provide cues in the potential environment which he is creating which might serve as foci for these new activities or suggest them. He may even be able, as Mackintosh did for the modern movement, to set forth in design ideas and suggestions which may then directly influence a society's aesthetic and, through that, its whole *Weltanschauung*. But even this is far from architectural determinism: and the first conclusion is that architects should be more modest and realistic about their ability to change the world through design.

The second conclusion is that architecture should be considered more carefully in relation to other factors that contribute to the total environment. This point applies particularly to town planning. It seems to me that this is the *leitmotiv* of Jane Jacobs's critique of American planning practice. For the main point of her book is that, instead of razing great areas of American cities to the ground and injecting 'cataclysmic money' into massive and deadening rebuilding projects, planners should think about what might be done to encourage the process of rehabilitation which is undertaken, in places like Boston's North End, by the people of the district in the teeth of unsympathetic planning departments and credit-houses. It was similarly expressed in the report which I prepared for the Basingstoke development committee on the social aspects of town development, which began by proposing social unity and social vitality as the main social objectives of such a scheme and went on to suggest ways in which the pattern of social administration and the people themselves who would be moving into the town, *as well* as physical design, could jointly contribute to the achievement of those objectives.

The adoption of this viewpoint leads, I believe, to a reappraisal of the sociologist's role in the design process. At present, I suspect, sociology is regarded simply as a method of inquiry, as tantamount to 'doing a survey'. The sociologist, then, is thought of *à la* Geddes, as the specialist fact-finder who provides some of the specifications of a 'mass' demand to which large municipal building projects must be tailored. That this is too limited a view comes out very clearly when different groups of consumers take different views about the design of the same kind of building. Brian Wells, for instance, in a study of the Co-operative Insurance building in Manchester, discovered that office managers preferred large, open office spaces while supervisors and clerks preferred smaller spaces; and that both groups could produce good organisational reasons to support their preferences. If a social survey were all that were required, than the sociologist's task would end there. But, as Wells points out, he must go on to examine what consequences large and small office-areas have for social attitudes and behaviour and to relate this analysis to the functions for which the office, as a social organisation, is set up. In this sense, Wells concludes, 'organisational and management problems will become part of the architectural and design problem'. Social theory is concerned precisely with these questions of social organisation; and sociologists and social psychologists have at their disposal an increasingly sophisticated theory as well as the methods for analysing organisational structures. They may thus be able to contribute more fully to the elucidation of design briefs. Their contribution, however, would be the more valuable if it were based upon a clearer understanding of how physical design, people and patterns of administration interact to produce whatever we might mean by 'total' or 'effective' environments. If it is agreed that determinism is a most inadequate makeshift for such an understanding, then the somewhat critical tenor of this paper may perhaps be accepted as a positive step towards the development of a more fruitful and creative partnership than presently obtains between architecture and the social sciences.

Social Theory
and the Total
Environment

The concept of 'environment', as it is now being used by planners, is clearly ideological. This came out sharply in Ann MacEwan's spirited review of D. J. Reynold's critique of the Buchanan Report, which appeared in the *Architects' Journal* in October 1966. To Reynold's claim that town planning was a matter of framing plans 'in broad quantitative terms' and thus the proper concern of economists, geographers and mathematicians, Miss MacEwan replied that planning was also a matter of *qualitative* concern with 'the creation of environment for human activities'. The Buchanan Report itself had defined an environment area as one 'having no extraneous traffic, and within which considerations of environment . . . predominate over the use of vehicles'; and it had spoken of environment in terms of 'the general comfort, convenience, and aesthetic quality of the physical surrounding for living'. Clearly, this concept implies the architect-planner's defence of certain kinds of general social value as against the more specifically technical considerations that tend to be the primary focus of interest for the economist and the engineer.

Architect-planners, however, use the term in an extended, and rather ambiguous sense. They are interested, they say, in the 'complete' or 'total' environment. Perhaps it is unfair to take this usage too seriously. It may, indeed, mean nothing more than physical design. Lewis Womersley, for example, recently addressed the Architectural Association on the subject 'Architecture as a complete environment'. By this, though he nowhere defined the terms, he meant simply the visible, physical environment: 'I have said hardly anything about the smaller but vital components of the complete environment (he said) – the importance of good design in pavings, seats, fountains, sculpture, trees, litter bins and signs. . . .' But his partner, Sir Hugh Wilson, appears to imply rather more than that in saying that 'if planning is concerned with the total environment, with the creation of towns of quality and character, *and with the well-being of people*, then I claim to be a planner.'

This genuine social concern – even social idealism – is one of the nice things about architect-planners. But they are often inclined to suppose that the design of the physical environment—which is their particular *métier* – will automatically secure the social ends which their idealism leads them to desire. This has often resulted in their adopting a set of assumptions that can be called 'architectural determinism'. This theory, more implicit than explicit, supposes that architectural design has a direct and determinate effect on the way people behave, and largely ignores the social factors that also affect environment and which a properly-formulated theory of 'the total environment' must surely incorporate.

The theory finds its classic expression in the neighbourhood unit concept. This concept was advanced in America in the early nineteen-twenties as a means whereby physical amenities could be systematically related to population, with particular regard to the safety and convenience of pedestrians, especially children. It was a rational solution to a problem of *physical* design. When it was taken up in Britain after 1944, however, it came to be regarded as a general panacea that would also meet the *social* criticisms that had been levelled at the housing estates built between the wars. Of these, the two major criticisms had to do with the lack of amenities and the absence of neighbourliness and a sense of community. It was supposed that, since these social virtues had been found in slum streets where amenities like pubs and churches and corner shops were also present, neighbourliness was fostered by the existence of such amenities. Accordingly, if a neighbourhood unit were similarly equipped, the residents would be equally neighbourly. As I have argued in the previous chapter, any plan that sought to achieve these social objectives would have to be concerned with the design of the social as well as the physical environment if it were to have any chance of success.

Social organisation and architectural design

The application of this point to architectural design can be illustrated by two simple examples. First: there are broadly two ways in which research students' and supervisors' rooms can be allocated in university science departments, which could well have implications for the way the departments were organised. An arrangement by which students' rooms were allocated *around* those of their supervisors would be the physical design counterpart of a colleague-like relationship between faculty and students; while a more formal relationship would have as *its* analogue the separation of their rooms at opposite ends of a corridor. The pattern of social organisation may even have relevance for the allocation of internal drainage-pipes. In a large teaching hospital, for example, each floor is occupied by a separate academic department. These may be drained either by horizontal ducts leading to one or two vertical pipes or mainly by verticals. Suppose the first alternative is chosen and that access to the ducts was from the ceiling of the department below. Then, one day, the pipes are clogged or burst. Clearly, the relationships between the two departments will be aggravated in a way that would have been less likely if the drainage had been by vertical piping.

These examples, both culled from actual buildings, are not intended to argue that social considerations should, or even can be paramount in design; but only that physical design cannot be considered without a prior analysis of social organisation. This, of course, is what is often attempted in working out a design brief; and usually it is taken for granted that the client – an industrial firm or a university, perhaps – knows enough about his organisation in a common-sense fashion to be able to spell out his requirements fairly simply for the architect. But we now have ample evidence to show, first, how difficult this process actually is; and, second, how little thought managements themselves give to the problems of social organisation in their establishments. Since the analysis of such organisational problems is an important aspect of the work of social scientists, it is likely that they could fill a very useful role as a kind of go-between in the design process.

The analysis of the social environment has been particularly well developed in the field of organisational theory, which has benefited chiefly from the detailed study of industrial plants. An organisation is defined as a social unit 'deliberately constructed and reconstructed to seek specific goals'; and organisation theory seeks to give an account of how such units work and, more specifically, of the social conditions that are appropriate for achieving different kinds of goal. There is by now a considerable literature in this field, but the illustration that seems particularly appropriate here is the study of *The Architect and his Office* which was published by the RIBA in 1962.

The study-group investigated how work was organised in sixty architectural offices. They discovered that in one set of offices, managerial authority and design initiative were centralised in the hands of the principals, while in the other set they were dispersed. In the former, the principals maintained a high degree of personal control over the work of the office and were unwilling to devolve responsibility or to ensure job-continuity among their staff. In the latter, co-operative group working was the norm; 'discussion, meetings, criticisms, etc. . . . went on at all levels' and the maximum degree of responsibility was devolved.

The significance of this distinction is that different performance standards were found to be associated with different patterns of organisation. The accompanying table shows that, in large offices, employing between fifty and 150 architectural staff, a better standard of design and technical efficiency was found where the organisation was dispersed. That these offices also had a low turnover of staff was due to the fact that the architects employed there worked in 'a well-informed and democratic atmosphere' and had a shared sense of responsibility for work done. Though the report noted that this atmosphere, and the wide-ranging discussion which characterised it, had less than the expected results on productivity, it also acknowledged that this was probably an important factor in the high technical and design quality of work done in these offices.

Work organisation in architects offices/performances of various groups

Performance Criteria	Centralised organisation		Dispersed organisation	
	medium-sized (8)	large (5)	medium-sized (10)	large (13)
Staff turnover	High	Average	Very low	Low
Staff salaries	Very High	Average	Average	High
Management efficiency	Adequate	Adequate	Mixed	Good
Technical efficiency	Adequate/ Good	Adequate	Good Good	Good Good
Quality of design	Good	Adequate	Low	R/A*
Profitability	High	Average		
Productivity (in terms of work certified)	High	Average	Low	Average

 * Almost all these offices were public authorities.
  Source: *The Architect and his Office* London: RIBA 1962, Table 56·1.

A further comparison of medium-sized offices employing between nineteen and fifty architectural staff revealed that both good design and high profitability could be achieved in centralised offices but only at the expense of very high salaries which did not prevent an exceptionally high turnover of staff. Indeed, the report points out a further, more subtle difference. For even these offices 'were rarely concerned with technical advance or profound studies, but appeared to depend rather on a previously developed technical vocabulary which they were good at exploiting'. The 'important contributions in the field of research and development in design and structural techniques', on the other hand, were produced by the decentralised offices of middle size which were 'a focal point for the growth of new ideas in the profession and the building industry'.

Such a differentiation in organisational structure has been shown to be highly relevant in several other recent studies. Burns and Stalker, for example, in their book *The Management of Innovation*, have drawn attention to the greater appropriateness of an 'organic' or decentralised organisation for technical innovation in industrial firms; and Revans's work on *Morale in Hospitals* suggested that a similar difference in the system of *hospital* management (and, in particular, the different patterns of communication which were found among the staff) might account for the fact that in some hospitals patients had to stay for twelve days after having their appendixes removed, while in others it was only eight. In the design of architects' offices or industrial firms or hospitals, accordingly, the organisational structure needs to be considered as a factor affecting the achievement of the organisation's goals. And since these kinds of structural differences have implications for architectural design, it is clear that social organisation *and* physical design need to be considered as complementary aspects of the total environment.

Social structure and town design
This conclusion applies equally to town design, in relation to which the concept of 'total environment' has probably been most used. Here again, the assumptions of architectural determinism are likely to show themselves. For architects are inclined to explain the different environment of cities uniquely in aesthetic terms. Certainly, the physical characteristics of site and architecture contribute to the environmental quality of Glasgow as much as of Edinburgh. But the social character of these cities is equally a factor in their environment. Glasgow's indictment of Edinburgh as 'East Windy and West Endy' is paralleled by the distinction between Manchester men and Liverpool gentlemen. The point of that still-valid difference is crisply revealed in nomenclature – in the contrast between St. George's Hall in Liverpool and the Free Trade Hall in Manchester, and between the *Royal* Liverpool Phil-

harmonic and the plain Hallé Orchestra. These reflect significant differences of social and economic structure between a Liverpool whose character was set by its patrician, commercial élite and a Manchester, originally less urbane, in which a manufacturing stratum was much more influential.

In the design of new towns, therefore, it is social structural factors of this kind, as well as the purely physical features, like neighbourhood design, that need attention in planning the total environment. In the United States, this is the direction in which thinking is now moving. One recent commentator, for example, has pointed out that 'one type of plan begins, not with the factory, but with designing *an environment capable of attracting* this leadership cadre of scientific, intellectual and skilled workers'. Michael Frayn in *The Observer* has also mentioned the American city which went about economic development by setting up an art gallery and symphony orchestra in order to attract distinguished scholars to the local university; who in turn would attract endowments and able students and thus entice to the area industrialists with plants needing steady supplies of graduate labour. 'So that', as Frayn succinctly put it, 'a small outlay on Bach and borrowed Botticellis would bring in a big return in new business.'

On a somewhat less ambitious plane, more rational procedures could be developed for estimating, say, the percentage of houses in town development schemes that could reasonably be offered for sale. In one large project of this kind the figure of 25 per cent appeared to have been reached by surveyor's 'hunch'; and this method is no doubt very widespread. But it is hardly the only, or necessarily the best method of assessment. A more systematic procedure, for instance, would begin from the observation that housing demand was influenced by social class, which, in turn, varied according to industrial structure. One might, therefore, start by establishing what, in the first place, a desirable and, secondly, a probable industrial portfolio might be for a new or developing town. From this, different occupational-class distributions could be derived from which inferences could be drawn more systematically about the proportion of housing which could be scheduled for sale. In this way, the social assumptions on which planning depended would be made more explicit and more precise.

However, it is possible that some of the social planning needed to secure the objectives that planners have sought to achieve by physical means may have only indirect implications for architectural design. This is particularly likely to be the case in the field of community organisation in which a much more sophisticated social theory is required to underpin social practice. We might try to find out, for example, why one town is socially vigorous and another comparatively dead; or why Coventry seized while Southampton muffed the opportunities for good planning in the immediate post-war period. Do different patterns of local government organisation have an effect in fostering or inhibiting the social development of towns?; or, more specifically, can any differences in performance be discovered, comparable to those found in studies of industrial organisation, between community centres whose administration is highly centralised and closely controlled by an education authority, and centres like those in Essex, for example, whose administration is comparatively decentralised? One can at present only put the question. But an attempt to answer them would have considerable relevance both for community theory and for the applied problems involved in actually designing the urban development.

There are certainly signs of a converging interest in the question of how physical and social design interlock. This is clear in Gropius's conception of 'total architecture' and equally in Doxiadis's notion of *ekistics* as the science of human settlement. It seems to be developing particularly in the United States. There, the Federal urban renewal programme of the last dozen years has led to the conviction, recently expressed by the head of the Housing and Urban Development Department, that 'Today urban renewal must deal with human renewal as well as physical renewal'. The same idea has permeated the development of Columbia New Town near Baltimore, which began with the preparation of a report on the planning of 'physical facilities and social processes' and which has appointed a director of *institutional* (not just 'social') development. It finds expression in Jane Jacobs's interest in the social and physical dimensions of diversity in *The Death and Life of Great American Cities* as well as in the counterpoint of 'mass culture' and 'the urban dwelling' around which Chermayeff and Alexander constructed *Community and Privacy*. Finally, in the ideas which have recently been advanced by Howard Perlmutter in *Towards a Theory and Practice of Social Architecture*, and by Milton Esman of Pittsburgh University and his colleagues who are beginning to talk of 'institution-building', there is an extension of organisation theory which, in its 'inter-weaving of theory, practice and reality certainly sounds like architecture, physical *and* social'.

No doubt this kind of thinking will in time have its effect in Britain, in clarifying the relationship between sociology on the one hand and architecture and town planning on the other. Planners and architects tend to suppose that sociology is *primarily* a method of investigation rather than a set of theoretically-based arguments. Understandably so, since sociology in their eyes has been represented by Patrick Geddes and, more recently, by the influential work of the Institute of Community Studies. The Geddes's *credo* of 'survey before plan' has been particularly congenial to our English empiricism. But while empirical inquiry is clearly essential, its direction needs to be governed not only by the immediate and detailed demands of planning practice but also by a more genuinely theoretical interest. Organisation theory, which has such an interest but is also manifestly relevant for managerial problems, offers the paradigm of the kind of social theory that would be most appropriate for planning; while the concept of 'the total environment', ambiguous though it presently is, affords a useful focus for collaborative effort between those social scientists, architects and town planners who are particularly interested in social development.

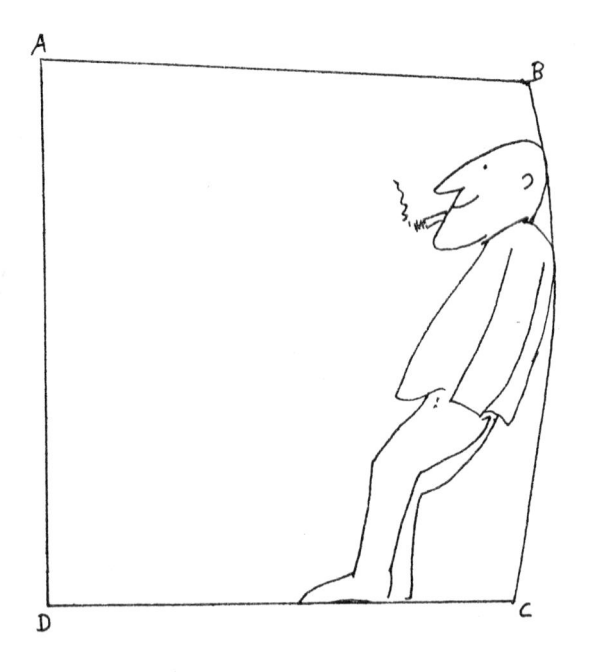

Community Power
and Voluntary
Initiative

My interest in this subject started a number of years ago when I began working on a study of how the Corporation of Glasgow designed and built its new housing estates and how it dealt with the variety of voluntary associations, ranging from tenants' associations to the Church of Scotland, which made representations to it about the social development of estates. In working out the line of thought which that inquiry provoked, I have come into close contact with a number of voluntary initiatives in various parts of the country which are trying to contribute a responsible and informed civic voice to the improvement of their local communities and I shall in due course be commenting upon how their efforts have been received by their local councils. The evidence of this kind of activity which is provided by bodies such as the Chilterns Society or the Woodley and Earley Society in Reading, means that the British tradition of voluntary enterprise remains as vigorous as ever.

In the last fifty years, however, we have moved from a situation in which charitable and voluntary enterprise in the field of social welfare was only just beginning to be supplemented by statutory provision, to the present time when, substantial and important though it is, voluntary social service operates alongside, and in association with a system of widespread and increasing statutory provision which costs annually something of the order of £4,000 million to maintain. This has obviously modified voluntary service. Some voluntary bodies have clearly been more sensitive than others to the changing patterns of social needs and of statutory provision and more flexible in adapting their activities to changed circumstances. Some have certainly fallen foul of the twin dangers 'of hanging on too long or of relinquishing absolutely'. If voluntary activity is still operating on something more than sufferance from a statutory authority that really believes it could do the job better (except that that would be an additional charge on the rates), then it is doing so because it has succeeded in finding something to do which the State cannot or will not do, either at all or as effectively.

The changing pattern of voluntary service has not so far been studied at all closely. It has to be acknowledged that it is very difficult to spell out precisely what has been happening, since the basic data – particularly lists of local organisations and details of their activities – are difficult to assemble. Lady Morris, however, has made a helpful analysis of the data contained in *Voluntary Social Services*, the directory issued by the National Council of Social Service, as a result of which she has been able to show that voluntary organisations have come to be 'more and more concerned with the needs of particular age-groups . . . and of the physically and mentally handicapped . . . (and have been) paying increasing attention to community planning and the provision of opportunities for better living'. In an address which she gave to the National Federation of Community Associations in 1957, she noted that 'social action for the provision of opportunities for better living . . . has been the avowed aim of more than half of the main voluntary bodies formed in the present century'. Of the 200-odd organisations founded between 1900 and 1951 which were listed in the NCSS directory for that year, 110 were concerned with education, recreation, housing, town planning and the provision of amenities: they were bodies which sought, in Lady Morris's words, 'to provide opportunities for people *to learn and do things together* or *to take action in the interest of the neighbourhood*'.

In the last ten years or so, this tendency seems to have been given a very considerable fillip by the setting up of the Civic Trust and the Consumers' Association. The effect of the Civic Trust has perhaps been the more direct, in the sense that, since it was founded by Mr. Duncan Sandys in 1957, it has led to such a resurgence of vitality among amenity societies that by 1964 their numbers had increased from 213 to over 460 and have now reached about 630. The influence of the Consumers' Association on voluntary organisation is less direct since it is mainly supported by individual members. But the fact, that since it was founded by Dr. Michael Young, also in 1957, its membership has grown to over 500,000 and that the Advisory Centre for Education and the Research Institute of Consumer Affairs have also come into existence on a similar basis shows how speedily it has developed. In addition to its individual membership, this consumers' movement has also produced a number of local consumer groups and has no doubt suggested the idea of consumer research to many voluntary associations with other specialised interests. At all events, there has been a notable upsurge of bodies of this kind in the last few years. Perhaps the most striking of them is the Confederation for the Advancement of State Education which was started by a group of Cambridge parents in 1960 and now has over 100 branches and a national secretariat.

I am myself directly acquainted with a number of groups of a similar kind, chiefly in the field of town planning. In Basingstoke, for example, a study-group was formed in 1961 under the aegis of the Workers' Educational Association to prepare a report on the social implications of the town development scheme. In Southampton, a very lively group came into existence to campaign for an alternative to the corporation's proposal to erect parking meters in the city and it has now transformed itself into a 'Buchanan study-group' to consider the implications of Professor Buchanan's report for the planning of Southampton. In Kent, the Bromley Design Group came into operation to promote good design in the town, while twenty miles away, in Maidstone, the newly-established Council of Churches brought together a widely representative body of citizens to conduct an enquiry into how the social services in the town might best be developed to meet changing circumstances. It is extremely difficult to find out how many similar groups have come into existence in the country as a whole. But the fact that councils of social service in Rugby, Hampstead and Preston have also, and quite independently, been carrying out similar inquiries suggests that this kind of critical function, involving first-hand investigation, the preparation of reports and the judicious appraisal of local circumstances is now becoming increasingly important in voluntary bodies, and is thereby reinforcing the tendency to which Lady Morris originally drew attention seven years ago.

There is a further thing to notice about this trend. Dame Eileen Younghusband has pointed out that there have been three main strands of social service in Britain: the tradition of personal service to the afflicted, the tradition of mutual aid, and the tradition of social reform. Though a great deal of personal service is still undertaken voluntarily, this is an activity which has largely been taken over by the State which now plays a major, and even an increasing role in this field. Furthermore, though the evidence for saying so is not absolutely convincing, it appears to be the case that the traditions of mutual aid and social reform are now growing in relative importance in our society. This is suggested by the fact that the more recently-developed voluntary services for the afflicted are organised, not by the middle class, as charitable undertakings for the less well-provided, but largely by the afflicted themselves. Bodies like the Infantile Paralysis Fellowship which was founded in 1939, the British Epilepsy Association, the Spastics Society and the Muscular Dystrophy Group, founded in the early 'fifties – you might almost call them the Christmas card societies! – were founded 'by the sufferers themselves, or by their friends and relatives, in association with members of the medical profession and other interested people'. Gone are the days when the middle-class exorcised its social conscience by organising the Charity Organisation Society for the relief of the poor. Epilepsy, muscular dystrophy, infantile paralysis and paraplegia may strike at children of *any* class; and though no doubt mainly organised, as before, by the middle class, these new societies bring people together in an *equality* of suffering and distress, quite different from the relationship which social welfare societies of earlier years sustained with those whom they helped.

What, in the present context, is particularly interesting about these newer organisations is the emphasis they place upon inquiry and publicity in addition to providing a service. Indeed, though they begin with the aim of providing a 'fellowship' among their members in which experiences and difficulties can be shared and thus more easily borne, it seems that these other activities come to assume as great, if not greater importance in their strategy of service. The work of the voluntary organisations which deal with physically handicapped children, for example, has grown to include 'informing and influencing public opinion on the nature and significance of the disease or disability; influencing legislation and the statutory provision of services on behalf of the handicapped; encouraging research into the causes and treatment of the disease or disability; and (finally) promoting the welfare of members, by direct provision of services, or by advice and help in utilising existing services'.

Thus the emphasis in voluntary enterprise has changed. From the viewpoint of the social worker and the social work tradition, voluntary societies tend to be regarded chiefly as agencies of beneficent action, dispensing material support, kindness, advice or doses of casework, as appropriate, to the unfortunate and the needy. And so, in a way, they obviously are. What I am suggesting, however, is that they should nowadays be seen increasingly through another set of spectacles provided, not by social work, but by a more philosophically-rooted political and social theory. In these terms, voluntary organisations are seen to have a crucial role in *assessing* the society in which they find themselves, in defending minority interests and concerns against the bull-dozing of organised power, and in providing a medium through which opinion can make itself heard on matters of civic importance. This is to see voluntary bodies less as casework agencies than as well-informed pressure-groups: and that indeed is clearly how these newer associations conceive themselves.

Voluntary initiative and community power

The effective embodiment into social practice of ideas spawned by voluntary initiative necessarily brings voluntary enterprise directly into contact with community power. The weakness of a pluralistic approach, which stresses the importance and virtue of voluntary groups within the State, is that it frequently fails to take political power seriously enough. This is equally true of much social-work thinking which, taking the individual as its focus, sees him, socially, as belonging to, and influenced by a family and other small groups, but ignores the fact that he is also a political animal. The implications of this limited outlook were brought out in the Home Office report on *The Organisation of After-Care* where a memorandum of dissent, which was accepted by the Home Office, criticised the majority report for being so concerned with casework problems that it ignored the necessity for the centralised organisation and direction that would be essential if the proposals were to be made effective. It came out, again, in John Spencer's book *Stress and Release on an Urban Housing Estate*. 'It is (he said) a common assumption of local community projects that the primary focus of attention is the local community itself.' Professor Spencer's at times painful experience of the Bristol Social Project led him 'to question the idea of the local community and to see neighbourhood relationships within the wider framework of the city. Local policy is closely bound up with central policy and decisions. . . . To effect change at the level of the neighbourhood' – the project set out to strengthen *local* initiative and leadership – 'it is necessary to begin work at the centre of the city'. It is, therefore, not enough to point out what a good thing voluntary initiative is and how vigorously it is flourishing. We have also to take account of the fact that voluntary action, to be effective, has to operate within a system of community power which, in this country, is at once more comprehensive and better supported than voluntary enterprise itself: a system of community power which can either stimulate or stifle voluntary activity.

Unfortunately, the relationships between statutory and voluntary agencies have hardly been studied in detail and I cannot claim to do much more than review what limited data I have been able to find.

One thing can be said, however, quite unequivocally, and that is that voluntary social service, voluntary enterprise of any kind, whenever it is referred to on public occasions, invariably receives an ecomium, as a distinctive attribute of any society that presumes to call itself democratic. Listen, for example, to Lord Beveridge, writing in 1948: 'The vigour and abundance of voluntary action outside one's house, individually and in association with other citizens, are distinguishing marks of a free society.' The following year, in the course of a debate in the House of Lords on voluntary action for social progress, Lord Pakenham, speaking for the Government, asserted that 'the voluntary spirit is the very life-blood of democracy'. At the annual general meeting of the NCSS in 1962, Sir Hector Hetherington made the same point in saying that voluntary service was 'one of the indispensible expressions and instruments of the spirit of a free society'; while the Joint Parliamentary Secretary to the Ministry of Health, in 1963, reiterated the belief that 'voluntary social service is one of the greatest glories of our British tradition'. Furthermore, as Madeline Rooff noted in her book *Voluntary Societies and Social Policy*, parliamentary legislation for social provision, by enjoining local authorities to 'secure the provision of' or 'to make arrangements for the purpose of' doing this or that, rather than obliging them directly and simply to provide the service, at least keeps the door open for the statutory authorities, if they chose, to collaborate with voluntary bodies in social welfare provision. All in all, then, we appear, formally at least, to approve of voluntary enterprise.

But when one comes down from this rather ethereal realm of credos and legal formulae and begins to look at what actually happens, the picture becomes a good deal more confused. All that can be said for certain is that there are some areas in which the voluntary creed, if I may call it that, is simply not part of the accepted pattern of beliefs, and others in which it manifestly is. Sir Alfred Owen made the point clearly at a conference held in 1963. 'In Staffordshire (he said) the voluntary organisations are recognised as part of the team by the council although not by the municipal boroughs who seem suspicious of them and fear that they are taking to themselves work that should be properly done by local authorities.' However, we have too little information, even of an impressionistic kind, to go on. It is impossible to say whether the authorities are generally favourable to voluntary enterprise or not, whether county councils, like Staffordshire, generally tend to be more sympathetic than smaller authorities, whether party-affiliation makes any difference: in short, we lack evidence. All that one can honestly say is that some authorities are encouraging and helpful, while others are not.

The response to circulars 7/62 and 18/62

Perhaps the quickest way of getting to the nub of the matter is to look at the way in which the statutory authorities reacted to the proposal contained in the 1962 *Hospital Plan for England and Wales* and the two subsequent Ministry of Health circulars which urged local authorities to foster greater collaboration and consultation with voluntary agencies in the development of their health and welfare services. In 1963, the then Joint Parliamentary Secretary to the Ministry of Health, concluded his inaugural address at a conference on community services for health and welfare with the customary salute to the value of voluntary social service before stating, in effect, that voluntary organisations were merely the passive tools of statutory policy. 'It is (he said) for the local authorities to establish what the gaps are that need to be filled and to say what services they expect from voluntary effort. . . . It is for voluntary organisations in their turn to mobilise the resources and to fill these gaps: they will be all the better equipped to do so when the need is shown to them plainly and the machinery for close and constant consultation has been established at every level and not merely at the top.'

Now that is what might be called a typical administrator's view of voluntary organisation. Though it talks of consultation, it is clear that this consultation precludes the discussion of policy, and that it was not intended to take the voluntary bodies into a genuine collaboration in the development of common interests. It is obvious that this kind of consultation is little more than a technique for winning goodwill and easing the way of a plan already formulated and presented as a *fait accompli* to the voluntary agencies. It is manifestly the central government's duty to specify the general direction which the development of health services should take, and no doubt, in practice, voluntary bodies *would* have an opportunity to contribute their ideas to the elaboration of policy. But this would be against the grain; for as Mr. Braine stated the matter, the voluntary societies are simply regarded as useful and passive providers of services to fill the gaps designated by the State, without so much as a say about *what* administrative gaps need filling or how these inadequacies, which they are expected to help to ease, might best be met.

In the subsequent discussion, the counter-argument came out very clearly. Mrs. Green of the Bradford css made the point that 'voluntary organisations often know of gaps which *local authorities* could meet and the identification of gaps and planning to fill them should be a combined operation'. Sir Alfred Owen asserted that 'voluntary service is not only there to fill the gaps left by the statutory services' but that it had a most important role as a pioneer initiator in the development of social services. In summing-up the conference, Dame Enid Russell-Smith judiciously sought to correct the impression given by Mr. Braine by stressing the need for a 'constructive cross-fertilisation of ideas' between voluntary and statutory bodies. But the layman might well be excused for having come away with the opinion that the Ministry really regarded voluntary bodies simply as convenient units to fit into plans drawn up by wise and omni-competent local authorities rather than as associations, frequently of considerable experience and ability, whose views might be solicited in the elaboration of social policy.

Some quantitative assessment of how the proposals contained in the *Hospital Plan* were received can be obtained from an analysis of the records of the Standing Conference of Councils of Social Service. These records cover fifty-seven mainly urban Councils of Social Service. The analysis shows that, though some useful steps towards increasing collaboration took place in a few areas, the general effect of the Ministry's suggestions was negligible. In a quarter of these fifty-seven areas no move was taken by either the css or the local authority to improve consultation; in a further quarter, the css *did* approach the local authority but with no result; and in a further third, while meetings were held, no further development was reported. In only one area in every six did any positive developments take place and in only three was the css accepted by the local authority as the co-ordinating body.

The factors in statutory reluctance

It is, perhaps, disheartening to rehearse these figures. But that is how things stand and we had better begin to ask *why* voluntary initiative of this kind should receive such short shrift from the agents of community power. The first thing to say, of course, is that there are many voluntary organisations which no town clerk or medical officer in his senses would touch with a barge-pole. Even a sympathetic critic like Miss Rooff has been obliged to point out that they are frequently conservative, parochial and so acutely sensitive of their independent status that (as the Younghusband report noted) they may even resent inspection by the local authority when acting as its agents, as if this were grossly unwarranted interference. In far too many quarters voluntary service is still associated with the belief that goodwill is an adequate substitute for efficiency and ability.

Now the plain fact is that officials and council-members are responsible for disbursing public funds in the best public interest and they cannot permit that authority and responsibility to be usurped. They are 'the custodians of the public purse' whose contents are always too small to meet all the claims that are made upon them. They must be accountable to taxpayers and ratepayers who have the right to know that their money which has been collected for public purposes is wisely spent. In giving support to a voluntary association, furthermore, an official of a local authority is also putting his professional reputation at risk. No public official can be expected to do that, and no council can be expected to support voluntary enterprise financially, without being persuaded that its credentials are sound and that it is going to be capable of responsible and effective action. For this reason alone, voluntary organisation needs to be trained and efficient; it needs, I think, to be para-professional. And the fact that many are not is one very good reason why, as a ratepayer, I am pleased to see statutory authorities exercise the greatest care in deciding which voluntary initiatives to back.

All that having been said, however, there are other, to my mind less creditable, reasons why statutory authorities are hesitant to collaborate with voluntary bodies. A local authority, like any other organisation, develops its own view of the world. Perhaps its chief danger is that of losing any real idea of what it is for: of elevating administration instead of public service as an end: of becoming limited in vision and constricted in imagination. In an interesting analysis from inside the Civil Service which appeared in *Public Administration* some time ago, Mr. F. T. Lockwood drew a contrast between what he called the 'governing' and the 'creative' mind in public administration. The 'governing mind' was solely concerned with getting things done as expeditiously as possible while the 'creative mind' was equally concerned with the values that the process of government subserved. He suggested that the 'governing mind' was at a premium in administration and that, this being so, inadequate consideration tended to be given to the broader questions of public policy and too much simply to keeping the wheels of administration turning smoothly. To be concerned, as a city medical officer or a county planning officer, with non-official voluntary groups calls for a pretty wide sympathy beyond the immediate demands of the job and professional interest. To quote Miss Rooff again, 'Professional workers, or laymen with wide interests, are not to be found in every locality, nor are local administrators always interested in activities beyond their immediate duties. Councillors may be wholly absorbed in party loyalties and exacting committee work. An MOH may be interested mainly in infectious diseases.' In my own limited experience of local authorities, the distinction has forced itself upon me between the town clerk, for example, who is simply a legal and administrative officer, and the corresponding official in some adjacent borough who can see what he is doing as a professional man in a wider context of civic purpose and with a wider sympathy for the unofficial side of his borough's life. But because men like that, whose professionalism is in perspective, are in the minority, there are far too many places where voluntary enterprise is regarded with less than the sympathy it deserves.

This lack of sympathy with voluntary enterprise, however, is only one aspect of a more general characteristic of local government. The report of the Royal Commission on Local Government in Greater London made the point clearly enough in one short and pithy sentence: 'The desire of the experts (except the very good ones) to get as far away as possible from amateur control, administratively and even physically, is a factor to beware of.' One can well understand why when one looks at many of our local councils. For while everyone has met aldermen or councillors of the very highest calibre and ability, the average run of our elected representatives is not particularly inspiring. Far too often, town councillors are inadequate to deal proficiently with public affairs. And many officials, suffering under the strain of having to submit to the frequently ill-informed criticisms of their political masters, whom they often have good cause to disdain, are reluctant to submit the work of their departments to still more public inspection and comment, and so become even less sympathetic to any attempt to make civic policies more intelligible to the lay public.

The evidence for these assertions is legion. The full council meetings at which the public are entitled to be present give no indication of what really affects policy decisions, while minutes, as we all know, are carefully drafted so as to reveal the least possible about the real meat of civic affairs. Though some authorities publish guide-books and reports, they rarely discuss the problems that actually face the council or explain the policies that have been adopted. As Bryan Keith–Lucas said in his paper on *The Councils, the Press and the People*, 'They do not invite the people to think about such questions as slum clearance and the development of the schools, nor explain what the Council hopes to do, and the difficulties involved. In fact, they do not treat the public as partners in the enterprise of improving or managing the town, but rather as strangers.' Towards the end of the war, the NALGO Reconstruction Committee put forward a number of suggestions for improving the public relations of local authorities, and a government committee also reported on the subject in 1950. However, as might have been expected, after a first flush of interest, little more was heard of these promising proposals.

Perhaps the clearest evidence comes from the field of town planning. While some authorities certainly go to some trouble to help and explain matters to applicants for planning permission, elsewhere the impression given is that of a 'bureaucratic machine which displays little patience and no kindness towards the individual applicant who does not understand "planning procedures" '. Planning proposals are usually presented to the public as *faits accomplis* and the exhibition of town maps and models, far from being an opportunity for the public discussion of principles and policy, is designed 'to impress and convince that what has been done is right'. If it had not been for a premature press conference which fortunately roused public opposition, there is little doubt that the original plan for redeveloping Piccadilly Circus would have been passed without a murmur. But a more recent and telling instance of how the public is disregarded in administration was when the Minister of Power decided to allow the Electricity Generating Board to run a supergrid power line on 160-foot pylons right over the Sussex Downs, thereby completely ignoring not only the objections of all the local authorities in the area but also the recommendations of the two Ministry inspectors who conducted the public inquiry. *The Municipal Journal*, as *The Guardian* leader pointed out at the time, is 'hardly an organ of excited or intemperate opinion': yet even it commented that 'it seems a fair assumption that these inquiries are being used only to give an air of democratic procedure to autocratic decisions.'

If statutory procedures are used in this way to secure what the administration wants, while putting on a veneer of democratic procedure by cynically sounding public opinion, it is not surprising to find that local officials, and to a lesser degree perhaps, councillors, are inclined to reject attempts on the part of civic groups to comment on or appraise, let alone to criticise, municipal policies. The reaction to such efforts can be illustrated from Southampton and Bromley. In Southampton a group of citizens got together in 1963 to present a case in favour of parking *discs* as an alternative to the meters which the Council proposed to put up. Two members of the group, a leading general practitioner and a business executive, prepared a very competent report in support of their case which the leader of the council agreed to place before its technical panel. How it was decided there is not known; but it was most likely ignored, as the corporation officials whom the group approached were a good deal less sympathetic and were notably reluctant even to give guidance on how to present the argument in the most acceptable way and what form of protest would be least offensive to the corporation. The attitude of the administration was perhaps most clearly indicated in the comment from one official that this group would prove to be no more than 'a fizzle-out'.

The reception which the Bromley Design Group received was almost identical. The Group was set up in 1963 at the instance of a local councillor who thought that a civic society might help to prevent Bromley becoming a 'dormitory-town hotch-potch'. Its members comprised architects, surveyors, town planners, teachers and journalists. They came to the conclusion that the plan for widening Bromley High Street which was then being considered by the council should be looked at afresh in the light of the Buchanan Report and they accordingly prepared an alternative set of proposals as a basis for discussion. The reaction of the borough engineer was to argue, firstly, that the Buchanan Report was not relevant to a scheme for widening the main street of the town and, secondly, that it was in any case virtually impossible to amend it as the plans were well advanced and had already been approved by the Ministry of Transport. A councillor made a direct attack upon the Group in the local newspaper by accusing them of being politically inspired and of 'sloppy thinking', while expressing his astonishment that it should be proposed to scrap a scheme for which the town had been waiting for more than twenty years.

What can one conclude from these incidents? Firstly, that, though expressed a good deal more discreetly, the reaction of these two local authorities to these initiatives was, in essentials, identical with that of the vice-chairman of the Plymouth planning committee at the Town and Country Planning Association's Conference in 1963, who attacked my paper (on a similar theme to this) with the cry: 'Your local planner needs not to be a sensitive ear listening to the townswomen's guild or the chamber of commerce and this, that or the other. He needs to be a single-minded steam-roller.' And secondly, that, though my later illustrations have come from town planning, these same attitudes inform local authorities' attitudes in many other spheres. Indeed, in seeking to develop closer collaboration and consultation with local authorities one may well come up against exactly the same assumption that the local authority alone is adequately qualified to undertake all the services within its domain and requires perhaps a little cheap help from the voluntary bodies, but certainly no advice or criticism from them or from anyone else.

The arguments for persevering

I may be wrong about many local authorities and many particular statutory departments. But, even supposing some of my comments strike home, how this disposition is to be met is a matter on which corporate experience is worth much more than anything that I, as an academic, can possibly say. But I may conclude, usefully perhaps, by suggesting *why* efforts should continue to be made to win over the statutory authorities to a more sympathetic view of voluntary initiative.

In the first place, neither local authorities nor voluntary organisations are all as good as all that. The 'official' view of the relationship between statutory and voluntary bodies seems to imply that the local authorities alone are competent to judge where the extension of services is most needed; and it is obvious that many local authorities would like us to believe that. But the calibre of local authorities depends on the quality of the officers and members who can be attracted into their service and this is by no means uniformly high. Even capable men, men with vision and imagination, frequently find circumstances weighted against them. The county surveyor of Lancashire recently noted that fifteen years ago he recommended that 907 miles of major roads needed to be built in the county by 1980 but that half-way on to 1980, less than eighty-eight miles had actually been constructed. Lesser men than Mr. Drake have certainly been known to give in, to lose heart under such circumstances. But even where senior officials do not give in to discouragement, they are frequently oppressed by the sheer weight of detailed administrative work which leaves little time for, if it does not completely inhibit, the breadth of thinking and the vision which are particularly badly called for in a period of rapid social change. Professor Fogarty has made the point that applies equally well to local government that ministers, top managers, trade union leaders 'have over-committed themselves to settling detailed problems and as a result have left themselves with too little time and energy to deal competently with the broader issues of overall government and management'.

The point I am making is that civic officials cannot be always expected to be omni-competent. That is why civic bodies with a voluntary membership whose task is investigation, appraisal and criticism are necessary and desirable adjuncts to the statutory services and not mere nuisance groups, as many officials and councillors appear to suppose. That is why, in Basingstoke, it was the study-group organised by the Workers Educational Association that until quite recently had done the most effective thinking about the social implications of the town development scheme; for both the development officials and the borough council were overladen with planning and building the physical fabric of the growing town, with a depleted staff and with new administrative difficulties to face. By the same token, it was the Council of Churches in Maidstone and not the statutory agencies which produced a report on the future development and co-ordination of the social services in the town. In both these cases, it was voluntary bodies of actively concerned citizens which took the municipal initiative.

The second argument is that the present electoral system itself biases the representation of opinion in the council chambers. In the first place it tends to frustrate the expression of minority opinion. An analysis of the London borough elections in 1964 showed that, in East Barnet and Friern Barnet, the Conservatives took seven seats with 11,000 votes, the Labour Party five with nearly 7,000 but that the Liberals, who had 100 votes more than Labour, got no seats at all. Secondly, the party system rules out of court many people of talent and ability who do not wish to be committed to a particular party, who do not find political party activity congenial, but who may well have a great deal to contribute to the civic life of their communities. It is admittedly difficult to see how a large council could be run effectively without party organisation, and I do not necessarily wish to decry what is often, and I believe wrongly, called 'the unnecessary incursion of party politics into local government', but I think we ought to be much more sensitive than we are to the disadvantages of a political system which excludes so many capable people from local influence.

This point is met, of course, by the general power which local authorities have to co-opt on to their committees. But this power of co-option is very rarely used except for education committees, on to which the Ministry of Education obliges local authorities to co-opt outside members. At national level, the institution of the life peerage gives an opportunity for precisely this kind of opinion and expertise to make a contribution to public affairs, while the use of advisory committees and the practice of consultation with specialised bodies (such as the Automobile Association and the Royal Automobile Club on motoring matters) allows for the injection of specialised knowledge from outside the party machinery. Local authorities, however, no doubt because they are nearer the ground, so to speak, and therefore so much closer to and less well shielded from the more outrageous pressure of local opinion, seem much more reluctant to adopt similar procedures. As Helen Roberts discovered in Birmingham, while civic officials 'were prepared to take seriously the suggestion that the churches might have a contribution to make to their work' in the field of social welfare, they were unwilling 'to draw the churches into partnership at the planning level of their work' and 'saw no need for consultation with the churches, except occasionally, on an *ad hoc* basis, if an issue came up which had an obviously "religious" aspect'.

Understandably, and properly, local councils are aware that their policies ought to be 'in the broad public interest' and that sectional interests should not be allowed to distort this concern – such as it is – for the common good. Fair enough. One does not wish to see councils so unstable and disorientated that they become little more than the spokesman for the chamber of commerce or the trades council or that they respond indiscriminately to the puff of every wind of sectional interest. A good council needs its own criteria for formulating its priorities and policy. But the belief that its mandate justifies its view that it is the *only* legitimate agent of the public interest, is weakened, as John Mack has argued, by the fact that local elections, at the best, are very formal affairs in which only a minority actually votes. Nor does it follow that sectional interest is invariably inimical to the wider public interest. An extra-mural class of ten members is a minority interest in all conscience; yet we deem it in the public interest to support such classes by giving them, in effect, a 90 per cent subsidy. What we have a right to expect from our councils is that they defend themselves from any attempt by sectional interests to usurp their freedom of debate and decision, but that they should seek much more actively and sympathetically than they do at present, to encourage the contribution of ideas and projects and criticisms from outside the party system. Responsible social criticism will never be congenial to more than a small minority. That is why it is precious and needs badly to be encouraged.

There are, happily, grounds for a restrained optimism. I think a lead in improving public relations is emerging in town planning. The planners are increasingly conscious of 'the general attitude of suspicion tinged with contempt' with which they are regarded. They are also inclined to believe that the people should be closely associated with the plans that are being made on their behalf. These two factors, together with recent American experience in this field, are beginning to make planners increasingly interested in the possibilities of citizen participation in planning schemes. Ling at Coventry and Shankland at Liverpool are two leading planners who are moving in this direction. Professor Buchanan, too, in his presidential address to the Town Planning Institute in 1963, stressed the necessity in planning for 'voluntary pressure groups of all kinds to "till the ground" of public opinion'. As a result of the Franks Report, furthermore, a number of changes were effected in planning procedure in the late 'fifties which obliged planners to make the reasons for their decisions more explicit. The citizen, one might say, is slowly coming to be treated as an intelligent and reasonable being.

Much the same point is embodied in Professor Brotherston's recent address to the Keppel Society on the development of general practice. 'In the long run (he said) an educated public opinion is the most powerful weapon for improvement in the (health) service and therefore the most powerful ally of the (medical) profession.' Already 'the expectations of the more educated and articulate patient now coming to hospital' had had 'some influence on thinking about hospital surroundings'. That comment, really, is the cue to my final point. We are rapidly becoming a more educated nation. More and more children are staying on at school and for every two places in institutions of higher education now there will be five by 1980. For those of us who teach in universities, especially, this expansion is a very considerable challenge, but it is one which is well worth accepting for the traditional political reason that the more educated the citizen the better equipped he is not only to exercise his democratic rights but also to foster the welfare of the community. It is now a sociological commonplace that the more educated contribute proportionately more in voluntary enterprise than the less: so that the educational expansion we are now facing seems likely to presage a growth in voluntary initiative and in the ability of people to act critically in their communities. And I suspect that they will also be less ready to accept the kind of local authority attitude which I have been criticising in this chapter.

We operate, of course, in a society which seems to regard education as valuable primarily for economic reasons rather than for what it has to contribute to *civic* life, to the life of the *polis*. The Engineering Industries Association, for example, recently urged voluntary support for educational institutions 'in order that they can make a maximum contribution to the progress of the nation's industry and commerce', while in 1964, at the British Association meeting, Sir Harry Pilkington was speaking of education as 'a profitable investment' in a 'product' who must repay the investment in 'work, productive work'. Now of course they are right, in a way; we need highly trained engineers and chemists and the like. But men are more than their jobs, and in focusing on education primarily as a kind of training for a job, we stand in danger of producing people who, like many town clerks, are trained to the law, but cannot by any stretch of the imagination be called *educated* men; men who are capable of transcending 'the limitations of their professional vision'. We stand in danger of producing people for jobs, and forgetting that they are also going to be citizens: and it seems to me all-important that those of us who are concerned in education and in community development should make this point as strongly as we can in the teeth of the current trend to regard education as something that has a value only in so far as it serves economic ends.

We may well expect, then, that the more educated, in the more leisured society which is coming, will wish and will be equipped to play a more substantial role than they play at present in appraising and assessing the society in which they find themselves and in contributing to its welfare. To this extent, voluntary initiative may be expected to flourish and increase and I fancy it will be much less disposed than at present to take for granted the arrogance and presumption of many of our local authorities. But before community power will acknowledge the claims of voluntary initiative, voluntary enterprise, for *its* part, must show itself to be much more efficient and capable than it frequently is at present.

Social Change and Town Development

The adjective 'social' always appears to be singularly imprecise by contrast with comparable terms such as 'economic' and 'political'. To the English ear, 'the economy' is undoubtedly real. It is the twentieth-century Mammon before whose demands we are prone to bow the head and bend the knee, acquiescent and unquestioning. So, too, is 'the State' real, as something to be suspicious of and against which to defend ourselves. But 'society' is very often regarded as a mere residual: as an indescribable hotch-potch of everything else from delinquent gangs to the mums in Bethnal Green: a confusion beyond analysis, beyond calculation: an amalgam of individual volitions at once arbitrary, whimsical and inscrutable. No wonder, then, that the title 'social change' should sound so forbidding and so vague. One can sympathise with the *cri de coeur* of Mr. Amos, Liverpool City Planning Officer, at a recent Conference of Urban Research Workers, who said that 'town planners frequently find themselves in the position of being expected to produce environmental improvements to achieve social aims which they cannot define, by techniques which they cannot test, for societies whose changes they cannot forecast'.

Demographic and sociological factors in planning
But the planner is not without his defences. For *his* purposes what is socially important is the relationship between those attributes of a population that can be measured statistically and the amount of space required to cater for them in the most convenient and economical form. For the planner, then, the basic 'social fact' is population structure – its size, age and household pattern – and the space-requirements that such a population will engender. So, with Nelson's eye to the telescope, the planner in point of fact ignores those indefinable social aims and unpredictable social changes about which Mr. Amos complains and

concentrates, as he must, on making provision for what he *can* predict. However desirable it may be for him to be acquainted with what Mr. Amos calls 'the common characteristics which unite people into each identified group', the relevance of all this for the drawing-board is marginal. Thus, for most town-planning purposes 'social' virtually means 'demographic'. It does not mean 'sociological' in the sense of being concerned with the character and quality of social relationships as such.

I draw attention to this quite crucial distinction at the outset because I propose to ignore demographic changes in order to comment more particularly on those changes in our social system which appear to me to be affecting the quality of our social and, indeed, our political life; and to consider what influence they may be expected to have on town planning in the next ten years or so. Mr. Amos, later in his paper, made the point that the planner 'needs to know those habits and characteristics which are not so much the product of social aims as the consequence of imposed conditions'. I am sure that, as a planning official, he is absolutely right. But for my part, I am particularly interested in the new social aims which are now being developed in our society and which are likely to affect not so much *what* is done on the drawing-board as *how* it is done, by refashioning the social context within which town planning is at present conducted.

I am very much aware, having said all that, of a wee professional gremlin shrieking out that the planner *ought* to be concerned with the sociological as well as the demographic dimension. And I am sure that many planners, whose spark of social idealism has not been extinguished in the service of a planning bureaucracy, squeezed between the minister on the one side and the large property-developer on the other, will find this as disturbing a starting-point as some sociologists who perhaps have a vested interest in this field. But I stand my ground. For if the planner's idealism leads him to wish to produce a good or a better society, his job is to design a physical structure that is convenient, economical and, if possible, well-proportioned; and I am not persuaded that the relationship between this physical form and the creation of a better *society* is anything more than extremely indirect.

The supposition that physical design can make a better society, in some other sense than one that is more convenient and economical to live in, derives from a theory of architectural determinism to which, in the many years that I have now spent in the love-hate relationship that sociologists tend to enter into with idealistic town planners, I have frequently noted that they subscribe. Some physical forms, it is true, do have determinate social consequences. But the most that physical design can do, sociologically, is to set conditions that are favourable or unfavourable to particular social activities. The circulation of the new senior common room at Southampton undoubtedly facilitates the conduct of conversation and argument that is the hallmark of a good academic staff. But what it is sometimes difficult for the architect or planner to remember is that the kind of conversation and the tradition of disciplined argument are given independently of design; and that no amount of good design will make up for the absence of a good academic tradition or make a town of dead-heads anything more, socially, than a town of dead-heads. In arguing this way I do not wish to pooh-pooh the sociological interest which the good planner brings to his work. But I do wish to suggest that it may be quite as usefully directed to analysing the conditions within which planning takes place as to analysing sociological consequences of physical design.

The changing pattern of voluntary action
It is from that standpoint that I have approached this topic. And I propose to start by commenting upon one social change that has been going on quietly and largely unrecorded during recent years; which may at first sound rather trivial by comparison with the many more obvious changes of which I shall presently speak but which is likely to make its impact felt upon the practice of those aspects of social administration which, like town and country planning, impinge so directly upon the individual citizen and our civic life.

We are witnessing, at present, the reassertion of the importance of the ordinary citizen: the development of what Professor Galbraith has called 'countervailing power' weighted against the vast oligarchies of our time. Within the sphere of national administration, the setting up of the Council on Tribunals in 1958 and the establishment of a Parliamentary Commissioner are part of this trend. In relation to the economy, the setting up of the Consumers' Association in the late 'fifties began a movement which has found a very ready response and which has subsequently been enlarged by the establishment of the equally successful Advisory Centre for Education and, still more recently, of the Research Institute of Consumer Affairs.

This main strand in the development of 'consumer participation' in Great Britain has been complemented by a galaxy of more specialised and smaller voluntary bodies, which have sprung up piecemeal in recent years to bring together people of like interests for mutual help on a voluntary basis, in order to establish services not yet provided by the statutory authorities or to complement and improve statutory provision by representing the interests and opinions of consumers. I think in particular, of bodies such as The Spastics Society, the National Society for Mentally Handicapped Children, the Muscular Dystrophy Group, the Infantile Paralysis Fellowship, the Patients Association, the Pre-School Playgroups Association, the Association for the Advancement of State Education; and there are many more besides. Most, if not all of those which I have mentioned have been set up in the last fifteen years, three of them since 1959, and they have grown at a formidable pace. The Spastics Society, for example, which grew out of two bodies founded in the early 'fifties, now has about 150 branches while the Pre-School Playgroups Association which was set up in 1962 has succeeded in establishing more than 120 groups up and down the country.

Elsewhere in the national scene there are clear signs of a revival of interest in voluntary organisation. In 1962, the National Council of Social Service heard Sir Hector Hetherington address its annual general meeting on the role of the voluntary services in contemporary Britain, and it convened a subsequent meeting to discuss the training of voluntary workers in social service. At about the same time the Ministry of Health was urging local authorities to foster co-operation and to consult with voluntary organisations in the health field. In his address, Sir Hector expressed his fear that the present situation might induce a 'weakening of the sense of personal responsibility, the feeling that in face of the vast forces now being deployed in the arena of national and international action, the individual is helpless'. The evidence of recent years, however, seems to me to argue the opposite case. For in this unexpected fashion, the lie has been given to those who supposed that the extended social welfare provision afforded by the State since 1945 would render voluntary enterprise and voluntary societies redundant.

Voluntary action, of course, is nothing new in Britain. It goes back over 150 years; and in organisations like the National Trust and the Civic Trust it has developed in unique directions which our continental neighbours come to Britain to see by way of compensation, no doubt, for all our planners and designers who always seem to be pestering them for ideas! This tradition comprises two distinct strands. On the one hand, there has been the humanitarian middle-class tradition that has inspired innumerable campaigns to improve the lot of the underprivileged and downcast: a tradition of compassion for others expressed in the Fabian movement and Voluntary Service Overseas no less than in Wilberforce's campaign for the abolition of the slave trade. On the other hand, there has been the tradition of co-operative *self*-help: a predominantly working-class tradition, designed for their *own* protection and improvement, which gave birth to the friendly society in the seventeenth, the building society in the eighteenth and the co-operative society in the nineteenth century. In the second half of the twentieth century, what seems to be happening is that the middle class is adding to its traditional concern for others a lively concern for its *own* welfare in an ever more complex and centralised society. It is developing organisations that are designed both to provide some kind of service and to appraise critically what the ordinary consumer gets from the economic machine and from the public services: organisations whose initial development owes much to the cordial publicity they have received in the columns of the quality press and whose chief weapon has been, of all things, the research report!

Social change and the middle class
This change of emphasis in the relationship of the middle class to voluntary organisation is not fortuitous. I believe it is related to more fundamental changes in our social structure. To that extent, it is likely to be more than a passing phase in our social development. Of these changes, the most immediate seems to me to be the fact that since 1945, notwithstanding the many non-statutory forms of social welfare from which Professor Titmuss has recently shown them to benefit, the middle class has become more dependent upon the statutory social services. Since the National Health Act of 1947, for example, the vast majority of people are on what used to be known as the doctor's panel, whereas, before the war, there was a sharp distinction between panel patients who were predominantly working-class and middle-class private patients. In the field of education, the number of places available in private schools has not kept pace with the increasing size of the middle class. The consequence of this is that the increasingly large middle class has, since the war, come into a new and closer relationship with the statutory services and thus finds itself appraising not just this particular doctor or that particular school but a national system of public provision from which its contact had hitherto been shielded by the smoke-screen of private medicine and private education.

Now the activity of responsible social criticism is not congenial to more than a minority. Most of us for most of the time are content to remain complacently acquiescent in our social niche. We busy ourselves with our routine affairs and look no further than our daily bread. The activist, the social critic, the reformer will always be a small section of any society. Their activities require not only the extra effort which few are willing to expend but also the ability to criticise and organise which comparatively few possess. These dispositions have always been found proportionately more among the middle than among the working class. Lady Morris's recent study of social enterprise has shown that even in a town like Halifax, in which perhaps only 20 per cent of the population are white-collar and professional workers, that stratum contributes 61 per cent of the membership of the voluntary societies and 71 per cent of the voluntary workers in them. In a large Glasgow estate of 50,000 people which I studied myself, the 5 per cent of the population who were white-collar workers contributed a quarter of the leaders of political parties, tenants' and community organisations. Observations of this kind have tended to obscure not only the fact that there is also a viable tradition of working-class leadership but that community leaders are a minority in whichever class they are found. They are, in a sense, the civically-educated minority; and this critical minority is steadily growing in size as the middle class itself expands.

The growth of non-manual employment is one of the main social by-products of the rapid process of technological change which is taking the economy by storm. This process and the economic development which it has brought about have set in train a demand for increasing numbers of highly-skilled personnel. Year by year, it becomes more difficult to find a job as an unskilled labourer, let alone keep it when once it is found. Year by year, more and more training comes to be needed for more and more jobs. The professions grow in number and increase in size; new technologies spring up; and the numbers employed in primary production on the shop-floor or at the furnace decrease relatively to those who don white coats for the lab or white collars for the office. The proportion of white-collar workers employed in administrative, technical or clerical posts in British industry rose from 8·7 per cent in 1924 to 19·2 per cent in 1958 and by 1967 had already reached over 25 per cent of the labour force.

This change in the social pattern, together with the new affluence which has accompanied economic development since the war, has led some commentators too glibly to the view that the working class as a whole is merging its identity in the middle class. Ferdinand Zweig, for instance, has recently argued that 'working class life finds itself on the move towards new middle class values and middle class existence'. It is true, of course, that many working class people are now earning as much as many in the lower middle class, and that in terms of material prosperity there is a growing similarity between them. But affluence does not change a man overnight. It does not easily disturb long-rooted beliefs and attitudes and assumptions. It does not suddenly make it easy for the manual worker to change over from using a pass-book at the post office or the savings bank to signing a cheque-book at Lloyd's or Barclay's; or to move over from the public bar to the saloon; or to learn to say 'table-napkin' instead of 'serviette'. There are no grounds for supposing that every well-to-do Midlands factory-worker taking home his weekly wage packet of twenty-odd pounds either aspires to middle class status or goes out of his way to achieve it. Nor can it be assumed that all the new-found office-workers have suddenly become attuned to middle-class living overnight.

The significance of education
Nevertheless, many have; and, what is more important, the pre-war middle class has been substantially augmented by many who have moved into it from the working class. In this transition, the role of education has been crucial. If at one time the ambitious working-class boy got up to university only by dint of hard graft, the schools' encouragement and his parents' sacrifice, nowadays the educational system operates more like an inefficient suction pump that is too small for the job. The increasing demand for higher education over the last decade has been born of technological change and nourished by economic prosperity. Technical development has put a premium upon education and paper qualifications as the key to economic and social advancement, while the facts that we live longer, marry earlier, have smaller families and are wealthier than our parents have made it economically possible for more people to support their children through increasingly protracted periods of education. The demand for higher education has grown beyond all expectation in the last ten years or so. Between 1953 and 1962, the proportion of children aged fifteen to eighteen who remained at school increased from 13·5 to 22·3 per cent: and the proportion is growing steadily, at the rate of 1 per cent per annum. At university level, there are now more than twice as many students as before the war and the demand for places is vastly in excess of supply. It is clear, therefore, that we are rapidly becoming a more educated nation and that this trend will continue whichever party is in office.

We are growing accustomed to think of education chiefly in terms of its value for economic development. 'The nation's economic future depends on education' cried the manifesto of the 1963 Campaign for Education; and it speaks straight to the hearts of employers who want better-trained staff, of parents who are unable to see that advanced education may be something more than training for a job, as well as to the teen-agers in the treadmill of 'o' and 'A' levels, for whom education is coming to be equated with examination, justified less by the excitement of learning than by the prospect of a good job in the future – the job with the desk, the phone and the slinky secretary of the advertisement page. We seem to be in danger of forgetting that education also has an importance for the community as a whole: that the well-educated man has a vital role to play as a citizen in society and not simply as a functionary in some economic hierarchy. So far, through such liberal education as still remains in our universities and the democratic practice of the seminar and the students' union, we have maintained this concern, and higher education has in fact served to provide a steadily increasing supply of active minds to the community as well as to the economy. The present educational expansion is therefore to be welcomed with open arms not so much for economic reasons as for the traditional political reason that the more educated the citizen the better equipped he is not only to exercise his democratic rights but also to foster the welfare of the community within which he finds himself.

However, the importance of educational advance for the development of social enterprise needs to be emphasised. In exactly the same way that economic growth depends on improving the intellectual calibre of technicians, managers and directors, so community development depends upon the degree to which intelligence, imagination and vision can be brought into play in community organisation. The significance of the educated minority, however, seems constantly to be underestimated. We give a great deal of thought to the very small minority in our society who are delinquent but very little at all to the much larger minority who can contribute something to social advance. The educated minority in any society is crucially important, for it is they who are most likely to make the significant innovations which will improve the quality of civic life, and make society a genuinely better place to live in.

The growth of a critical, educated minority is indicated in the remarkable increase in the circulation of the quality press which has taken place in recent years. Since 1937, the circulation of quality dailies has risen three times as fast as that of the popular press. Since the war, their readership has been growing even more steadily while the popular press as a whole has even begun to lose circulation. A similar increase has taken place in the demand for adult education. The fact is that education tends to be self-generating: that it is now precisely the educated who demand more education. In 1961-2, the record number of over 200,000 adult students, some 30 per cent more than only four years previously, enrolled for evening study-courses run by the universities and the WEA and by 1964-5, this number had risen to just under 220,000. These students were mainly from the better educated and professional middle class. The Workers' Educational Association, which began in 1903 as a means of taking university education to the proletariat, has now become an instrument of bourgeois enlightenment! The point which I am making must not be exaggerated. Adult education courses are patronised by only a small minority; the popular press is still the staple reading of nine people out of every ten. But it is evident that the educated minority is growing and will continue to grow. It will never be more than a minority. But it is a vitally important group, as I see it, because of the critical role which it tends to play in society and because of its ability and willingness to re-interpret old traditions of corporate action in relation to modern ends.

The relationship between this educated minority and political organisation, however, is rapidly changing. The process of government necessarily grows more centralised as the units of organisation (outside London and the county of Rutland) become even larger. The role which the educated citizen might theoretically be expected to play in local government has become increasingly time-consuming in the large authority and trivial and routine in the small. These are strong disincentives to active political life, and they have been getting stronger at precisely the time that the educated minority is increasing in size and when higher education, the traditional fodder of democracy, is growing in influence. What I suspect has been happening is that this growing critical minority in modern Britain, unwilling to tolerate the slowness and the caution with which local councils tend to move, unwilling to spend years in the lower echelons of political party machines waiting for influence, have been organising independently in voluntary bodies, where, for all their lack of resources, it is sometimes possible not only to pioneer new developments but also to represent the consumer's interests more easily and more congenially.

The role of the critical minority in town development

How, then, does all this relate to town development? The answer is that the vitality of our towns largely depends upon the kind of voluntary groups that bubble up within them. The local authorities may provide community centres and other facilities but this is of only limited value unless there are also groups which wish to use them.

Though buildings are clearly important, what is even more important is the sensitivity and thought which is given to encouraging community development in other ways: Swindon's excellent social development policy, for instance, or Coventry's readiness to allocate £1,000 to neighbourhood groups to enable them to deal with the more easily remedied complaints. But there is also a new role for voluntary bodies in town development which is to contribute to the planning process an informed and authoritative citizen's voice and to foster developments which the local authorities, overwhelmed as they often are by the task of building the fabric of a new town, with a constant eye on the local rates and the restrictions imposed upon them by ministerial economies, are frequently unable to effect. I believe that citizens' groups have an important role to play in doing some of the thinking and researching and stimulating which needs to be done if the social aspects of town development are not to be neglected, as so often they are. This kind of academic contribution is singularly fitted to the practice of adult education; and I propose to answer my question by briefly describing the work of the Basingstoke study-group on town development which has largely stimulated my reflection on matters of this kind.

The Basingstoke study-group was set up in 1961 on the initiative of the local branch of the WEA. Since 1957, when the first small development scheme was inaugurated, the branch had been interested in exploring its implications. So when the LCC plan for a new town at Hook was shelved and it was decided to expand the population of Basingstoke from 26,000 to 80,000, the chairman of the local branch approached Dr. Dunning and myself at Southampton University to see whether we would help the Association to consider what the larger scheme would entail. Out of this initiative there developed two study-groups. The one dealing with the economic aspects of the scheme published, under Dr. Dunning's name, an analysis of the economics of town expansion; while the sociological study-group of which I was chairman completed a report on the social implications of the scheme.

Innovation in conservative institutions like universities often depends upon doing something new while retaining undisturbed the old administrative structure. Administratively, this group appeared to be an adult education class in sociology and in a sense, of course, it was. But it operated in fact rather more as a research group seeking actively to apply its knowledge to the social problems involved in town development. From the beginning, members were accepted only on condition that they would contribute actively to the work of the group. For the first year, we pressed on with half a dozen members; at the end of the project we had sixteen. About half of them held university degrees and another quarter had professional qualifications as teachers or nurses. The group included an architect, a naval architect, an almoner, a housing manager, a research worker and a number of secretaries and executives in commerce and local government. It was, in my experience of adult education, the most highly qualified class that I had had the pleasure to tutor.

The point from which we began was to ask what we could most usefully contribute to the town's development, as a small voluntary group meeting through the winter for two or three hours each week. Though Dr. Dunning's study to some degree proved us wrong, we decided that such a group could not match the local authorities at their own game; that there was no point in our duplicating what the county officials might have been expected to be doing. What we felt we *could* profitably do, however, was to direct attention to the social and psychological implications of town development.

We had a number of reasons for this decision. First, it was less easy to quantify these aspects than the demographic aspects of town development; and in the absence of quantification, they tended either to be neglected because they were said to be too vague or to be over-emphasised particularly when issues like 'loneliness' and 'new town blues' were being considered. What was needed here more than anywhere was sound and dispassionate evaluation, and this, we believed, a study-group would be able to give. Our second point was that the voluntary associations, ranging from the Church to Rotary, had a crucial role to play in town development, both by way of easing the psychological and social disturbance which it would inevitably entail and in developing the quality of civic life, for which a town council can plan, but which in the end depends upon the ordinary people in the town itself to develop and foster. The trouble with such voluntary societies is that they frequently find it difficult to think constructively about their role in a rapidly changing society. Even if they are alive to the situation and have goodwill and ready helpers, their leaders are frequently so hard-pressed with organisational chores, so unacquainted with techniques of investigation and so ill-equipped with office staff that they are unable systematically to collect the experience that others have had in similar situations, or to pioneer new ideas except in a somewhat *ad hoc* and unsystematic way. It was clear, then, that a group such as ours could usefully serve the community by acting as a channel through which information and ideas could be systematically investigated and then pumped out, so to speak, to assist the voluntary organisations in the town to think out what the expansion might entail for them; and we believed that this role was the more important since we were beginning well before the start of the development scheme and could therefore hope to do some active thinking before the expansion really got under way.

In working out our ideas, we kept in mind the distinction between bodies whose primary task is to act and those whose task is to think; and we thought of our role as that of a catalyst seeking to produce information and ideas upon which *others* might act. Our aims accordingly were: (i) to work out in advance what social problems were likely to arise in the course of the development scheme; (ii) to find out how these problems had been met elsewhere; (iii) to furnish this information together with ideas for social action to the voluntary groups in the town and, where appropriate, to the local authorities; and (iv) to encourage such bodies to think out creatively what their role might be in the process of town development.

The work of the group was designed firstly to do the purely academic job of inquiry and secondly, to begin to get people in the town thinking about the future. We started off in the depressingly conventional way by doing a survey. The town had already grown by private immigration since 1955 and we decided to see how these recent newcomers had settled down by conducting a survey of nearly 200 households. This helped us to understand some of the problems we were interested in and gave us grounds for believing that the experience of people who had moved as individuals into privately-owned houses tallied in many respects with that of people who had moved out *en masse* under municipal schemes to out-county estates, overspill areas and new towns. For the second session's work we looked more widely at the experience of other developing towns, by reviewing a large number of articles and accounts. In our report we tried to relate this evidence to Basingstoke's experience and to argue out what might be done to minimise the social difficulties involved in the overspill scheme and to develop creatively the town's social and cultural life.

The other side of our work began in 1962, when we had ourselves something useful to say from our own inquiries. Or aim here was to get townspeople to think about what would be facing them in five years' time. An advisory committee was set up which received our first report with warm interest and approval; and the Hampshire Council of Social Service gave the group a generous grant to enable us to invite speakers to the town. With the financial support of the county council and the university, a very successful five-day study tour of five other new towns was organised, impressions of which were made public through the medium of the local press and a film. A one-day conference was also convened under the chairmanship of the Bishop of Winchester on the role of the churches in town development. What I found singularly encouraging was the fact that members of the group themselves, as local citizens who had made themselves well-informed on subjects like this, began to discuss these issues more fully with interested bodies like the ministers' fraternal and even gave a series of lectures on the subject at the request of the very active Towns-women's Guild.

Future development

It is along such lines that I particularly wished to see this work develop. Partly stimulated by one of our public meetings, a council of social service was eventually set up in the borough. What I should like to see would be the Basingstoke study-group serving that council and its associated bodies as a civic research organisation, providing an effective intelligence service in relation to the many social problems that the development scheme will bring in its train and constantly trying to think ahead to the new questions that are likely to arise as the town expands. Its work would be to publish, perhaps annually, a report on some aspects of the development and to seek out new ideas for con-sideration. In this way the adult education movement could begin to reformulate in the nineteen-sixties its original intention which was to be *actively* rather than passively related to a constructive social purpose, by becoming an instrument of *public* education and contributing directly to the developing life of an expanding town.

To some degree, what we are doing is still a bit 'in the clouds'. This is inevitable for we are still very much pioneering and though theory is reasonably clear, the details have to be hammered out in practice. I very much hope that this movement will grow. Not only does it represent a vital new departure in adult education, but it seems to me equally a new line in community development. British town planning, which began with the idea that it should be democratic, that the people for whom the plan was prepared should be actively associated with its elaboration, has become increasingly bureaucratised. Nowadays demo-cratic planning, for the most part, means no more than the reference to a local council, tempered by the public inquiry and the right of appeal. This cautious interpretation of democracy is congenial to many a planning official for whom daily contact with his political masters may well be so wearing and time-consuming as to make him shy off still more direct contact with the people themselves. It is equally congenial to many a local councillor who may like to feel that his alone is the power and most of the glory. But in terms of a wider democratic theory, it is most unsatisfactory, since it makes too little effort to engage the interest and support of the ordinary consumer, who tends to be treated either as a moron or else as a troublesome nuisance. My argument, essentially, is that the process of social change which we are experiencing is going to produce many more educated and critical consumers and that this is likely to force a change in the public relations of planning if the planners themselves do not change it beforehand. The work which began in Basingstoke is part of this change. It is, I believe, spelling out a new interpretation of the role of the educated citizen in a democratic society and that, in the long run, may be the most important thing about it.

The Idea
of Social
Planning

Planning is an amalgam of rationality and social idealism; and of the two it is rationality that underpins the idea of the city region. The concept draws attention to the disparity between the present-day pattern of urban government and the economic and social organisation that centres on, but now extends well beyond, the city itself. It is argued accordingly that administrative areas should conform to these realities. The argument is the more compelling now that physical and economic planning are coming to be more closely integrated, as the conception of the aim of economic policy changes. For instead of trying simply to maintain an economic balance within a region – a view that originated in the depressed areas between the wars – we now seek positively to promote economic growth. The argument of this paper is that a similar reorientation needs to be made in our conception of *social* planning if social idealism is not to be extinguished by the rationality of regional planning.

Conventional social planning
In Britain, the term 'social planning' does not have a clear meaning. Not only does it sound to English ears too much like State interference in the citizens' personal affairs, but what might be described as social planning is in fact undertaken by government departments which deal separately with schools and houses and the health and welfare services. Used in the context of town planning, the term carries with it the aura of the nineteen-thirties. Like the idea of economic balance, it is a retrospective concept, concerned with meeting the kind of problems that first engaged public interest in the inter-war municipal housing estates. It has to do with ensuring that schools, clinics and other amenities are not neglected in the planning of such estates; with relating such facilities to the size and structure of the population, and with trying to

avoid or alleviate the incidence of social disturbance in new residential areas. Important as these issues are, it is impossible not to feel that they grow out of a static and conventional view of social planning which, in the city region of the future, will need to be rather more attuned to a context of rapid social change.

This conventional approach to social planning derives in part from the fact that the professions concerned with this aspect of town planning have a singularly restricted view of what constitutes 'social'. Among economists, for example, the social context of economic planning still tends to be filed away as one of the many 'other things' that are conveniently 'being equal'. This solution has been less open to town planners. But for all their traditional concern with social values, planners have hardly had the occasion to develop more than a superficial view of social structure. For when planning is defined as land-use control, only those aspects of social activity are normally considered that are directly relevant to estimating how much space to allocate for particular purposes. Town planners, therefore, are chiefly concerned with demographic and ecological facts rather than with social institutions as such. Three-quarters of the section on 'the people' in a recent new town plan, for example, was devoted to population structure, employment and shopping, against a bare 5 per cent to 'community structure' which was chiefly a discussion of the neighbourhood unit concept. To the extent that planners have been concerned with general social well-being, they have either adopted some theory of architectural determinism which supported their belief that physical design *per se* would have a determinate and, of course, a desirable effect on social activity, or they have assumed that these matters would be properly dealt with by social development officers or social workers.

Even among these professions, however, a similar restriction of view is evident. The ambiguity of the idea of social development in British town planning is indicated by the fact that by no means all new and expanding towns have appointed social development officers; and that, even where they have done so, their departments have often become the dumping grounds for residual functions such as public relations, attending to groups of foreign visitors and collecting social statistics. As for the social services proper, their major focus is upon providing for the poor, the needy or the delinquent. Certainly there has been a transition from offering material relief to a more personal kind of service involving some sort of social casework. The social worker, however, typically deals with a client defined as 'a case', that is as constituting a problem in the sense of deviating from a social norm in a way

E

that disturbs the client or troubles the authorities, or both. And though it is called 'social' work, its emphasis is predominantly on helping individuals rather than upon understanding and perhaps seeking to change the social structure within which those individuals find themselves.

An implicit theory of government

The *common* element in these professional ideologies is a view of the nature of government and of the citizen in relation to it. They all share the assumption that the government's function is to provide a service for the people. And the cognate assumption is also made that the people, as recipients of that service, are – and perhaps should be – passive, inert and acquiescent in accepting the professionally-administered services in the conduct of which, for the most part, they can have only the most indirect say or involvement. This is simply to state what we presently mean by administration. Indeed, it is on these assumptions that the competence, general efficiency and broad impartiality of British government rest. These are no minor virtues; and the only reason for spelling out the obvious is that it is a good deal less obvious that these very assumptions are becoming increasingly anachronistic.

Our system of local government was effectively established in the nineteenth century, largely in response to the problems of the rapidly growing urban areas that developed in the course of industrialisation. The system had three main features. In the first place, it was chiefly responsible for providing physical services like streets, sewers and lighting and for preserving law and order. Secondly, there was a great disparity of status between the members and officers of local councils and those for whom services were provided. And thirdly, the ordinary citizen was very much a member of the *lumpenproletariat* – only a hundred years ago, still disenfranchised, uneducated and subject to extremely long hours of routine employment. Bagehot, writing in 1867, could understandably speak of his countrymen as 'a deferential people', while Lord Rosebery, thirty years later, depicted the new urban working-class as 'the heedless casualty of unnumbered thousands of men'. In such circumstances, it is equally understandable that the aristocratic-derivative pattern of a strong executive should have been confirmed and the notion that we – the government – had a duty to provide services for them – the passive citizenry – should have been institutionalised.

In the course of the last hundred years, these conditions have changed very considerably. Local government now is responsible for services that affect the personal life of the citizen much more directly. Our local authorities provide not only streets and sewers, but also education, recreational facilities, psychiatric and other social services. These demand for their effective prosecution the witting concurrence, if not the active collaboration of the citizen, in a way that the earlier services did not. The efficiency of a sewage system, for example, is governed chiefly by purely technical factors, whereas an educational system to be efficient also depends upon winning the active participation of the student in the process itself. Furthermore, with a quarter of the workforce in white-collar employment, the status disparity between the councillor and official and the elector is much smaller than it was, while such a population, increasingly well educated and apt, therefore, to participate more actively in affairs, is less inclined to passivity and acquiescence. How curious then that local government should still be conceived in nineteenth-century terms as the provision for a largely passive population of services chiefly designed to meet the problems rather than to encourage the potentialities of the people for whom the provision is made.

Failure to encourage human potentialities

One of the chief weaknesses not only of local government but of many of our British institutions at the present time is their failure to foster human potentialities. The contrast with American practice is particularly striking. Whether it be the populist assumptions of American government or the fact that manpower, at the formative stages of American economic development was in scarcer supply than in Britain, the Americans seem to be much more sensitive to this. To validate the point would need a study to itself. But it is significant that Mr. Fred Catherwood, the director-general of the National Economic Development Council, should have remarked that, for British students graduating in the United States, 'the marginally lower rate of pay in Britain was less of a deterrent (to their returning home) than the fact that jobs in Britain did not give them the responsibility sought'.

The attitude of university authorities to students illustrates very clearly this reluctance to encourage the development of initiative and responsibility. For the universities, in practice, often belie their claim to be training students to be intellectually independent and responsible. In one university, for example, it was only when the students boycotted the refectory that their request for a place on the university's refectory committee was finally admitted, so deeply embedded was the view that the administration provided a service for a passive *clientèle*. In another characteristic instance, a faculty committee was considering the problems that university expansion would entail. One or two members urged that students should be given every encouragement to do things (such as running a bus service to transport students lodging in outlying areas) which might help to meet these difficulties. Such idealism! When the minutes were read, this positive approach had been suitably adulterated to read: 'The Students' Union *might be able to assist in some of the matters* referred to.' These, of course, are small examples that can only indicate, rather than demonstrate the point. But the frequency of such attitudes, especially when shown towards university students, affords at least circumstantial confirmation of the view that a characteristic of British administrative practice is its tendency to undervalue, even perhaps to fear, the potential contribution of those for whom public services are provided. The main point of the present argument is that social planning in the city region must go well beyond the concept of providing a service and seek also to engage the human potentialities in the region in its *social*, as well as in its economic development.

Already in some fields of administration some such change of direction can be discerned. Widespread public education began in 1870 simply as a means of educating the new industrial proletariat. It was restricted to the useful subjects of reading, writing and arithmetic and the method of rote learning, aided by the cane, was consistent with that narrow view. Nowadays, the range of subjects is broader and the methods of instruction are more calculated to win the active interest of the pupils. Nowhere is the transition clearer than in mathematics teaching where the mechanical learning appropriate to the training of a ledger-clerk is slowly being replaced by the 'new maths' designed to encourage children to see the point of what they are doing and to foster creative thinking instead of stuffing them with half-understood facts. In the social services, too, there is a growing interest in the possibilities of preventive work which would help to set up conditions under which social problems would be less likely to arise, while casework is slowly coming to be complemented by community development work which is specifically based upon the idea of encouraging the members of a community themselves to deal with their own problems in their own way.

Citizen participation
Such shifts of direction are not easily accomplished; and the town planners' recent interest in citizen participation shows clearly the circumscribed manner in which a profession adjusts to new social realities. This interest in citizen participation grows out of the planners' dis-

satisfaction, first of all, with the actual results of planning. 'In this country', said Sir Hugh Wilson recently, 'we have built up on paper perhaps the best planning system in the world; and yet the visual results are dismal with but a few exceptions.' Secondly, town planners consider that they have a bad public image. Professor Buchanan, for example, has described the public's attitude to his profession as 'suspicion tinged with contempt'. The thinking which has been prompted by this dissatisfaction has led planners to conclude that the reason for their failure to gain the public's confidence and for the uninspiring output of the planning machinery is that they have been too remote from the lay public. The Americans, on the other hand, have developed a practice of 'citizen participation', particularly in the context of urban renewal projects. Let *us*, then take up 'citizen participation' in Britain, the argument runs, and all will be well!

Some planners give the impression that citizen participation is a kind of wonder-cure. Max Lock, for example, a well-known British planner, believes that this method will get 'surprisingly quick results' and that proposals which, 'under the usual bureaucratic procedure of facing the public with a *fait accompli* plan would take years,' would in this way win approval 'in weeks and at the most months'. One cannot but sympathise with a policy designed to involve the layman more fully in the planning process: anything that might improve the tarnished public relations of our local authorities is welcome. But it must be noted that the concept of participation masks the question: at whose initiative does participation take place? The idea, as it is presently being advanced, implies participation at the *planners'* behest. It is not thought of as participation on the initiative of the citizens in the design of their *own* environment, but as a means of facilitating the work of the planner himself.

Yet the public is showing that it also wishes, and is able to participate in planning on its own terms. It is challenging this emasculated concept of participation which is congenial to the professional but less than satisfactory to the active citizen; and finding that, when it does so, through highly competent civic groups like the Barnsbury Association in Islington, the planner, like the university authorities referred to earlier, is rather less than sympathetic. Officials and councillors alike, in their unwillingness to consider the schemes proposed by such groups on their merits, are simply reasserting the belief that the citizen should remain passive before the operation of the duly-appointed executive. Such a view is increasingly anachronistic. For it ignores the fact that nowadays associations of this kind may well be as professionally competent as the planners themselves and less disposed than earlier generations to be deferential and acquiescent.

Social planning of the future

The social planning of the future will have to take such facts fully into account. It will have to adapt itself to the changing society which is emerging from the impact of a highly advanced technology. We are so apt to think of the implications of this impact solely in economic terms that we ignore its significance for social organisation. A rapidly developing technology has the effect of increasing both the proportion of a labour-force employed in tertiary at the expense of primary industry and also of the highly-skilled and more educated manpower needed in the economy. Such a labour-force is more likely and also more able to participate actively in the wider community. From the standpoint of conventional administration, the initiatives which this will entail are likely to be regarded as a threat to professional autonomy as well as to the claim of an elected council to represent the general interest. This will show itself in the usual attempts to denigrate such activities, such as 'They're trying to teach their grandmothers to suck eggs' or 'They're merely a sectional interest' or, worse, 'Of course, they're politically-inspired'. Increasingly, such arguments will not do; and it will be necessary to develop a kind of social planning which will seek to discriminate between such initiatives and to encourage those which have something positive to contribute to the social development of the region.

The grounds for doing this are not simply that such groups are likely to become increasingly influential in the future. It is also that the objectives of social planning now ought to be expanded to include improving the quality of civic life, just as in physical planning we seek to improve the quality of the physical environment. The quality of civic life in a democracy has to do with the degree of social vitality – of active participation – in that civic life: and this is largely a product of what the citizens, through voluntary organisations, contribute. The kind of contribution that is made, however, may be affected directly by the kind of support which these organisations receive from the public authorities, by the willingness of those authorities not only to provide a service but also to encourage and foster local talent and ability and to engage it in the social development of the community. That is the distinctively new direction which social planning must take in the regional context.

Such a conception no doubt sounds vague and even utopian: inevitably so, being innovatory. But instances are not entirely lacking, though the theory is unformulated which might integrate them into a *general* view of social planning. The collaboration between the new town authority, voluntary associations and ordinary citizens to build the new Harlow sports centre, the excellently-organised arts festival at Hemel Hempstead, the swimming club at Southampton: these are examples of the kind of practice envisaged. Perhaps more typical of present British practice, however, is the fact that so few schemes have been developed that take advantage of the £4 per head of population which, since 1963, it has been possible to levy for social development projects in the new towns; and that this has mostly been because the development corporations, the public authorities and local organisations have been unable to find a formula for co-operation and finance.

Recent American experience, though by no means perfect, is nevertheless well worth considering. Social planning is found at both ends of the social spectrum – in dealing with the problems of the slums and in the development of a new town. In the slums, the 'poverty programme' was set up under the Economic Opportunity Act of 1964 in order to engage local organisations and the indigenous leadership in a programme of self-help in urban poverty areas. In Pittsburgh, for example, eight such poverty areas were designated and a mayoral Committee on Human Resources was established to co-ordinate the programme within the city itself and to act as a link with the federal government and an agency through which federal funds could be allocated to local organisations. One such committee was the Citizens' Renewal Council in Homewood-Brushton, which operated under a board of twenty-one directors elected from local residents and from representatives of business and industry operating in the area. It was at this council that proposals from local agencies to undertake projects in the area were initially considered, through the federal funds were made available directly from the Mayor's Committee to the agency concerned, which itself contributed a percentage of the cost of the project in kind through the allocation of premises or staff time to the scheme. In this way, a Presbyterian Negro church was funded to provide a psychiatric counselling service, the Urban League to set up a programme for helping pregnant schoolgirls and the Lutheran Service Society to establish a home-making programme, with the help of paid local volunteers.

The relevance of all this to British practice is, of course, limited by the fact that our system of public social welfare is better developed than the American. The poverty programme, furthermore, has been seriously criticised as inefficient, fragmented and inchoate, and also on the grounds that it was mere panacea that hardly effected the major changes that would be needed in the economic and social structure of the United States if the poverty and second-class status of the Negro were to be effectively alleviated. For all that, it constitutes an interesting attempt to engage indigenous leadership in the alleviation of local problems and is therefore worthy of consideration in this connection.

At the other end of the scale, the new town of Columbia, outside Baltimore, affords an interesting example of a town being designed around the question 'Can intelligent planning lead to new modes and patterns of behaviour that *increase the options for human development* instead of inhibiting them, as many urban environments do today.' Here, at least, is an active and witting concern for 'matching growth in numbers with growth in human personality, character and creativity'. The design implications of these ideas were originally worked out in an impressive report on the planning and programming of physical facilities *and* social processes which was prepared by a panel of consultants which included social scientists as well as experts in recreation, education and health. The details of the report, which was completed in 1964, may well be modified in the course of developing the town; and as it is only in the early stages of construction, it is not yet possible to assess the practical value of these ideas. Nevertheless, the setting up, in the early phases, of a division of institutional development shows the importance which the Columbia planners attach to this aspect of their work, while the idea that planning is concerned not only with physical design but also with making those social arrangements which would 'encourage and facilitate (note the terms!) the expression and fulfilment of the needs *and* aspirations of its citizens' indicates the direction which, in this country, we need to take with social planning in the city region.

Admittedly the political and social contexts within which American practice has developed differ so greatly from our own that ideas cannot be transplanted unmodified from one side of the Atlantic to the other. In particular, the fragmented and decentralised pattern of American government presents difficulties in co-ordinating planning which we do not have to face so acutely. Indeed, our physical planning is becoming increasingly rationalised, more and more integrated with economic policy. We can even envisage the development of the regional economic councils, weak though they presently are, into viable regional planning agencies. With the growth of a technologically-based society, whose efficient conduct demands this high degree of co-ordination, we also get a citizenry which is increasingly capable and desirous of making a positive contribution not only to the economy but also to the community. The argument of this paper essentially is that it will therefore become necessary *and* possible to make our increasingly centralised system of government more flexible and adaptable at the local level; and that the problem of *social* planning in the remaining decades of the present century will be to find a means whereby that potential can most effectively be engaged in autonomous social development, so that the rationality of planning may be complemented by the social idealism which is equally part of the planning tradition.

The Social
Aspects of a
Town Development Scheme

Basingstoke is a small town of some 30,000 people on the main line between London and Southampton. The town-centre focuses upon the crowded high street with its old coaching inn, upon the open-air market and the Victorian town-hall in the square and the distinguished mediaeval church down the dip of Wote Street. The character of this old North Hampshire market town, however, is rapidly changing. For to the north and west, the new factories, warehouses and housing estates are the signs of a town development scheme under which Basingstoke will become an industrial town of over 80,000 people by the nineteen-eighties.

This scheme was first mooted in the Greater London Plan which Sir Patrick Abercrombie produced in 1944. One of its chief objectives was to relieve the population pressure and housing shortage in London, not only by building new towns but also by encouraging the expansion of smaller towns, like Basingstoke, which lay well beyond the sprawl of the metropolis. The New Towns Act of 1946, therefore, was followed in 1952 by the Town Development Act. This legislation, designed to 'encourage town development in country districts for the relief of congestion or over-population elsewhere', gave the Treasury and local authorities the power to finance the development of any towns which agreed to accept people who were prepared to move out of the large conurbations. Soon after the Act was passed, the London County Council opened negotiations with Basingstoke which led, in November 1957, to the borough's acceptance of a scheme under which 12,000 Londoners would be moved into the town over a period of ten years. This initial agreement, however, was quickly overshadowed by the disclosure of the London County Council's plan to build a new town for a population of 70,000 at Hook, only five miles away. Hampshire County Council, as the planning authority concerned, opposed this project and put forward an alternative proposal to accommodate the same number of people by developing Basingstoke and two smaller towns in the county. This solution was agreed upon in October 1961 when the Hook plan was finally shelved; and it is as part of this scheme that Basingstoke will grow by the planned immigration of about 20,000 families, most of whom will come from London.

Unlike the new towns which are developed by government-sponsored corporations using government money, town development schemes are administered jointly by the local authorities for the 'exporting' and the 'receiving' areas. Other interested authorities may also be associated with such schemes as 'participating' authorities. The Basingstoke development is sponsored by the London County Council as the exporting authority, by the Basingstoke Borough Council as the receiving authority and by the Hampshire County Council as a participating authority; and a joint committee on which these three councils are represented administers the scheme through the Development Group, comprising the architects and other officials specially appointed for the task. It was for that committee that the following report was prepared early in 1964.

The object of this report is to set out as comprehensively and coherently as possible what major social issues are likely to arise in the planning and development of Basingstoke and, within that framework, to comment in greater detail upon a number of more specific topics which are involved. By the term social I have not meant simply either 'tenant reaction' or 'demography'. I have been concerned more particularly with the social *relationships* that develop between groups or categories of person within the community. In that sense the sociology of physical planning is concerned with how these relationships are affected by the disposition of physical amenities. Social development, on the other hand, has to do with the administrative processes and policies which are designed to make the best use of human resources, where 'best' means the promotion of what Dr. Nicholson, in his report on *New Communities in Britain* calls 'a full and satisfying life in the community'.

This desideratum needs to be spelled out more precisely at the outset, for it is in the light of such a criterion that planning and development policies must be appraised. It seems to involve two very general criteria: the idea of social unity and that of social vitality. The idea of unity has underlain the efforts made in many of the new towns to encourage people of different social classes to live in the same residential neighbourhoods. It has also found expression in the idea that the community centre should serve as the common focus of all local social activity 'without distinction of political, religious or other opinions'. It is now clear that these particular policies are generally unsuccessful in bringing together in common activities people of different social strata. Nor is this surprising. For such divisions are so deeply rooted in the economic structure of our society and so firmly reinforced by the educational system and by social conventions as to be influenced only marginally, if they are influenced at all, by superficial modifications of residential location and leisure-time activity which, in any event, are open to individual choice. But even if these particular policies have failed, the idea of social unity is not entirely irrelevant, for it stresses the desideratum that all residents, irrespective of social differences, should be encouraged to share some sense of identity in and some responsibility for the town and its welfare.

If the foregoing argument rests upon the assumption that social differentiation cannot be avoided, it does not follow that nothing ought to or can be done about it. What is particularly distasteful about status differences in any community is the way in which people use them to exaggerate their own virtues and to emphasise the faults of others. This is particularly true of rapidly growing communities where the new-comers tend to be regarded with suspicion and even antagonism, not only by the original residents, but by people who were themselves new-comers only a few years before. As the clerk of one 'overspill' authority has remarked, the biggest social problem with which he had to deal in his district was 'the latent hostility of an existing population to new-comers'. The ideal of social unity makes it necessary to try to minimize the growth of social animosity within the community.

The second criterion of social vitality has entailed the idea that a good town is one in which people participate responsibly in a wide variety of social activities. Here again, this desideratum has tended to be asserted too dogmatically and unrealistically. It has sometimes been rather uncritically associated with certain psychiatric notions and generalised into the quite erroneous view that people can only be men-tally healthy if they are actively engaged in social activities within their local society. But this is far too rash a view. For, while withdrawal from social contacts is certainly one indicator of mental disturbance, it is not the only one nor is it unambiguously related to mental ill-health. In any case, not everyone wishes to take part in social activities. Even in Crawley, where the voluntary associations are particularly vigorous, only 30 per cent of the population belongs to them. But if this view will not do for individuals, it is nevertheless most desirable for a *town* to support as wide a range as possible of social and cultural initiatives.

In the light of these criteria, then, the development of Dr. Nicholson's 'full and satisfying life in the community' seems to me to entail:
(i) that the townsfolk, irrespective of social differences, should feel a positive sense of identity with and responsibility in the town;
(ii) that the development of acrimony and animosity between the different sections of the population should be minimised, if it cannot be entirely avoided; and
(iii) that every encouragement should be given to the growth of a vital social and cultural life.
It is important to observe that the development of a community cannot be promoted successfully from outside or imposed by authority from above; it is the product of the uniting in a common enterprise of both statutory and voluntary effort. This seems to me to be so fundamentally important that I should regard it a necessary condition for achieving these social ends.

There are, accordingly, three factors that have something to contribute to the town's social development: (i) people, (ii) physical design and (iii) social administration. Many local authorities have been inclined to take the view that community development can be achieved by their action alone. From that standpoint, physical design and the adequate provision of social amenities have tended to be regarded as almost more important than the people for whose benefit they are provided. I put forward the alternative view that the major contribution to the 'full and satisfying life' is made by the people themselves. But clearly the statutory authorities have a most important role to play in so far as they control many of the conditions which can hinder or encourage the townspeople to make that contribution.

I THE PEOPLE: PROBLEMS AND POTENTIALITIES

Basingstoke has been growing rapidly for the last fifteen years. Since the mid-fifties its population has increased by over fifty per cent so that there is already a substantial proportion of newcomers in the town. They have mostly come as private individuals moving into private estates. By contrast, the movement of population into the borough in the future will be on a much larger scale, much more organised and more fully under the control of the statutory authorities. In many new towns it was hoped to get what was called a 'balanced' population, which meant a population similar in structure to the national one in terms of age and social status. This desideratum was invariably scuppered by the fact that industry preferred younger people and that it was in any case younger people who were most disposed to move. The population structure that a town will get, therefore, will be determined firstly by the kind of occupational demands that the incoming industries will make and by the readiness of people to come out to meet them.

Inducements to move

In the present economic situation it is clear that many more firms will be wishing to come to Basingstoke than can possibly be accommodated. The planners, therefore, will be able to exercise a choice among them and this choice will have direct effects upon the town's social structure. It seems most unlikely that Basingstoke will be able to avoid, even if it wished to do so, attracting a very high proportion of young people. Already, in the newly-built private estates in the borough, the proportion of householders under forty years of age is sixty per cent as against a national proportion of about thirty-five per cent; and the corresponding figure for families recently nominated by the LCC for housing in expanding towns was seventy-two per cent. But what the planners should be able to affect through the industrial selection procedure is the class structure of the population. As I understand it, there is as yet no formal selection policy; and it may well be difficult if not undesirable to formulate one explicitly. However, there seems every reason to expect that it will be possible to attract to the town a substantial proportion of commercial offices and even research organisations and thereby to increase the proportion of white-collar workers in the population. Thus, it is likely that the incoming population will be 'unbalanced' by containing higher than average proportions of young families and of the middle class. Since a good deal of the detailed planning of the town depends upon assumptions about the population structure, and since this itself depends upon industrial selection policy, it may be helpful for the Development Group to spell out in greater detail what a desirable and/or probably industrial portfolio would comprise, so that the demographic assumptions on which physical and social planning alike depend could be made more explicit and more precise. The value of a comparable analysis was very clearly demonstrated in the quite innovatory investigation that was made a year or two ago into the space requirements for retail trade at Cumbernauld.

How the industrial selection will in fact work out depends, however, upon whether workers of the appropriate categories can be attracted to the town. In some cases people will come at whatever cost either to improve their accommodation or to better their job. There appear to be significant differences between the classes in the reasons for wishing to move. A study of recent movement into Basingstoke itself showed that manual workers moved mainly to improve their housing while non-manual and professional employees did so chiefly for occupational reasons. It is probable that a high proportion of highly-skilled manual workers are sufficiently well-housed in London not to be induced to move in order to improve their accommodation; and the evidence from Swindon and Aylesbury and, indeed, from some Basingstoke employers suggests that this class of labour may well be very difficult to attract. There are also grounds for expecting that skilled workers in the engineering trades will be particularly loath to move from the London area where they are in a sellers' market. Some key workers, it is true, are likely to move with their firms. An LCC return showed that thirty per cent of the wage-earners housed in four of the expanding towns in the year and a half ending in July 1963 were long-standing (and presumably skilled) employees who moved with their firms. But special attention may have to be given to the possibility that workers of this kind may not readily leave the London area.

Though the problem may not be so acute in the case of professional and managerial employees, provided that career opportunities are satisfactory, these are people who are more mobile and for whom the attractiveness of the town and its environs as a place to live assumes a particular importance. Though the evidence for this is not by any means conclusive, it is possible that the satisfactions demanded of a new town are much more demanding among people of this class than among manual workers. Moving, as they do, less for housing than for occupational reasons, they may well derive much less satisfaction from simply possessing a new house than do manual workers who are more likely to have moved precisely in order to improve their accommodation. Accordingly, while people of all classes are attracted by a town with good amenities, this is likely to be a particularly important factor in attracting and retaining the professional and managerial employees and their families who, as I have argued earlier, may well constitute a higher than average proportion of Basingstoke's future population.

Social adjustment
The move out from London to Basingstoke is a social as well as a territorial transition: a shift, that is to say, from one social milieu to an-

other. Psychological stability tends to be fostered by social regularity. We are what we are, as persons, by virtue of the social relationships into which we enter and we are sustained as the persons we are by the conventions of the social groups to which we belong and by the assurance that comes from knowing implicitly how to conduct ourselves and what conduct to expect of others in specified social situations. Any change in these conventions or sudden introduction to new kinds of social situation, in which we are unsure of the relevant conventions, makes us feel uncomfortable precisely because the regularity of the social relationships is disturbed upon which our personal assurance is built. The move from one social milieu to another, therefore, puts people in a situation where they are at greater risk to psychological and social distress.

Recent discussions of these issues have properly drawn attention to the fact that many people moving out to new communities are leaving older urban areas with which very often they and their families have had long-standing connections. It has been suggested that the social malaise and psychological disturbance experienced by newcomers to housing estates is due largely to their having been winkled out of their closely-knit kin groups in very stable old communities. Though this may conceivably aggravate the upset of the transition, it is by no means the sole or necessarily the most important factor, since difficulties of re-adjustment are experienced by most people who move into unfamiliar surroundings. The problems of readjustment affect the husband and children of a family a good deal less than the wife, upon whom the major burden of rebuilding social contacts in the new community chiefly falls. In a study of a London out-county estate made some years ago it was found that the main nervous illnesses were neurotic reactive depressions among women; and recent studies in Crawley and Basingstoke have amply confirmed that it is the women who are particularly prone to depression and dissatisfaction in new housing areas. It needs to be added that this is for the most part a temporary phenomenon and that most people in due course settle in and adapt to their new environment quite happily. Nevertheless, since these transitional difficulties will affect everyone who moves to the town, and since a minority will find themselves at least temporarily overwhelmed by them, it is useful to state briefly what is here involved.

Social readjustment is called for in two main fields. People have, first of all, to establish a new domestic regime. In moving to a new or expanding town, not only the standard but also the cost of living, especially of the manual worker, is likely to rise. The rents of new houses are likely to be higher than he was paying previously while the price of foodstuffs and other commodities is frequently higher, especially in the early phases of development when the number of shops is limited and there tends to be a seller's market. Being young, the newcomers' families are usually growing and many are also moving into larger dwellings than they previously occupied. They are thus faced with the additional financial burdens of furnishing a new home. Since the move does not normally entail the promotion of the main wage-earner or necessarily increase his income, these increased costs are met either by credit, which in the working class generally means expensive hire-purchase, or by the wife's going out to work. Most people, of course, will certainly manage to re-establish a new pattern of domestic arrangements speedily enough, but there will undoubtedly be a small but less competent minority who are unable to do so.

The second and no less important area of readjustment is in the wider sphere of social relationships within the community. This involves contacts with neighbours and with local social activities. The incomers will be coming from many different parts of London; and while differences in rent levels will act as a kind of social sieve, segregating them broadly by income and social status, there will be in each new area a great variety of people from a wide variety of social backgrounds. In the intimate life of a residential neighbourhood superficially slight variations of behaviour and social standards can cause a good deal of upset, especially to the housewife, in the initial stages of development before neighbours finally settle down into a mutually tolerable code of conduct. Furthermore, many people find it equally difficult to re-establish membership in associations like churches or darts clubs which may have given them a great deal of satisfaction in, say, Walthamstow or Bethnal Green. It is important to appreciate that, for people for whom the move out to Basingstoke may well be the most momentous event in their lives, this re-establishing of social contacts may be a singularly difficult experience.

Enough is now known about these social processes for the phases of social adjustment in new communities to be specified quite precisely. For the first six months or so the newcomers are likely to be busy settling into and enjoying their new homes. During the next two or three years they experience the difficulties and tensions of adjusting to a new social environment, in the course of which many people either move back to where they came from or seek a transfer to another house, often on another estate. Thereafter, they begin to develop in a more stable and assured atmosphere a fresh set of social contacts and friend-

F

ships in the community. As far as I am aware, no thorough study has been done of the extent to which people return to London from the expanding towns, but in Swindon, some 10 per cent were said to have done so, and a comparable figure was given me by the managing director of a leading Basingstoke firm about the skilled workers which it recruited in the large industrial areas of the Midlands and the North. Some such movement is, I think, inevitable. But it is clearly a substantial diseconomy and for that reason, as well as on humanitarian grounds, it is desirable that efforts should be made to ease the shock of the initial transition.

Social differences

A second major area of disturbance centres upon the differences which exist between different sections of the community. People obviously classify themselves and others in relation to themselves. These classifications, for example, between the newcomer and the old-timer or between the well-off and the badly-off, are not figments of the imagination. They are real and unavoidable and they may be acrimonious as well. Already a slight touch of animosity can be discerned in relations between the incomers and the older townsfolk who are understandably resentful of the changes which the town is now undergoing. Such animosity does not need to be overt to be effective, for much subtler techniques of avoidance and rejection can make newcomers feel singularly unwelcome. In many places, indeed, the adjustment of the 'overspill' population to the life of the town into which they have moved has been adversely affected in this way and has given rise in one case to 'bewilderment, loneliness and sometimes fear'. These antagonisms sometimes produce more obvious social tensions when divergent interests of the two groups in the population find their expression in local organisations. It is to be expected that the residents' associations that have been set up in the borough will be complemented by tenants' associations, and it may happen that these bodies will in due course come into open and bitter conflict in a way that can only exacerbate the relations between these two groups in the population and hinder their mutual acceptance. In the same way other organisations, including the borough council, can come to be divided acrimoniously between conflicting interests. It is not possible to avoid divergent interests in a community, nor is it possible to cover them up. Indeed, I see no reason for regarding division of interests as undesirable, provided only that the conflicts which such divisions generate can be handled by both sides in a spirit of mutual goodwill rather than, as so often happens, of mutual distrust and dislike. This, however, cannot be legislated for: it depends entirely upon the exercise of restraint and good sense by the leaders of various groups within the community.

Leadership in the community

The number and quality of leaders which a community will produce is related to its class structure and the cultural traditions that permeate it. Though some ability to lead and organise is to be found in every stratum of society, it is found proportionately more among the middle than among the working class. Even in predominantly working-class estates in Glasgow, the white-collar workers contributed a quarter of the local leaders although they formed only 4 per cent of the population of the estate; and in Harlow, the social development officer has recently commented on the high percentage of talented professional people, and especially of teachers, upon whom the very vigorous communal life of the town has chiefly depended for its organisation. It is probable that the proportion of middle-class persons in the new Basingstoke will be similarly high and that their contribution to the development of the community will be proportionately great. There are, however, at least two *caveats* that ought to be made. First of all, the middle-class incomers may well be what have been described as 'spiralists', that is to say, executives and professional men who come to Basingstoke for a few years as one stage in a career pattern that takes them from one branch of a major company to another as they steadily ascend the spiral of managerial promotion. In such circumstances they may not be disposed to contribute substantially to a community with which they have no other links than that their firm happens to have an office there and which they will, in any event, soon be leaving. Secondly, such incomers may be inclined to take houses outside the town in the surrounding villages and to contribute little to the borough's social or cultural life.

As for working-class leadership, this has tended to be underestimated. There is a viable tradition here which finds its typical outlet in political and trade union activity and in sports and social clubs in the community. The characteristics of this tradition vary from one part of the country to another and it is difficult to discover what can be expected of the London working class in this connection. However that may be, the social development of the town depends upon engaging and encouraging local leadership wherever it is to be found. Many people, even in Basingstoke itself, are known to have taken on leadership responsibilities for the first time as a result of such encouragement and to have acquitted themselves extremely well in their posts. Some thought, therefore, deserves to be given to this whole question of how the leadership potential in the community can best be engaged.

II SOCIAL CONSIDERATIONS IN PHYSICAL PLANNING

Under this heading two main questions need to be considered: (i) what social facilities should be provided in the town and (ii) how they should be located. A good deal of discussion has gone on in planning circles since the nineteen-twenties about the social significance of neighbourhood development and I shall consider this topic after discussing the facilities that ought to be provided to meet the social needs of the growing town.

One of the major weaknesses in town planning since the war has been the inadequate or belated provision of such amenities. The reasons for this are obvious and understandable. In conditions of economic stringency priorities have to be assigned to different kinds of development and houses and schools are clearly more urgent than community centres and playgrounds. I suspect, however, that social amenities have frequently been regarded as mere 'frills' of development. But the effects of inadequate and belated provision of meeting places and other communal buildings are not easily eradicated and, as *The Lancet* remarked some time ago 'a few thousands of pounds spent on social amenities and social development may save hundreds of thousands used on therapeutic services and wasted in labour lost'.

The case for adequate provision for social activities is now greater than it ever was, for one of the main tendencies in modern living, to which the chief planner of the Ministry of Housing has recently called attention, is the increase in leisure. This fact, together with the increasingly wealthy and well-educated population of the future, will undoubtedly call forth a demand for more adequate provision, particularly for leisure-time activities.

The development of these amenities as the town expands will be undertaken mainly by the statutory authorities or by commercial interests, the one providing what is required by statute, the other what is profitable. The provision of schools by the local authority, for example, and shops, pubs, dance-halls, cinemas and bowling alleys by commercial interests can therefore be taken for granted. What needs to be given special consideration is how the other social amenities are to be provided which are neither mandatory nor profitable: amenities that are either exclusively social, such as meeting places or community centres, or which cater for minority, and notably cultural and educational interests.

The town centre

In the brief for the town centre development it is encouraging to note that it is proposed to make provision for a social centre and clubs. One of the chief lacunae in the town's social provision at present is a decent and centrally-sited hall in which public meetings can be held, and it is to be hoped that a hall or a suite of halls of different sizes will be provided in the social centre and in the new municipal buildings. A further desideratum would be the provision of convenient office accommodation, perhaps in or adjacent to the social centre, for the many branches of the voluntary social services such as the marriage guidance council, the family planning association, the citizens advice bureau, the Women's Voluntary Service and the like which will undoubtedly develop, no doubt in co-operation with a council of social service, as the town grows. However well organised such bodies may be, their service to the community is often less efficient than it deserves to be for being carried out in unsuitable and often makeshift premises scattered about the town. In view of the very important social service which they provide in areas outside the range of the statutory services and of the expectation that this kind of voluntary service will grow in importance in the coming years, such provision ought, in my opinion, to be given the most sympathetic consideration. The family centre at Stevenage, operated under the Stevenage Council of Social Service, in which administrative arrangements are shared among the different associations concerned, offers a useful example of what might be done in this connection.

Interest in the arts and in further education is increasing yearly. Statistics of the patronage of drama and music are difficult to get. But it is significant that, in spite of all the mechanical aids that encourage people to listen to music or drama in their own homes, and notwithstanding the development of educational broadcasting, the live theatre is flourishing and attendances at evening study-courses throughout the country are increasing at a greater rate than ever before. A town that encourages 'quality' activities of this kind is not only doing something intrinsically worthwhile. It is also building up its reputation as a good, lively and interesting place to live in, and this, at its crudest, is in a very real sense an economic asset equivalent, perhaps, to commercial goodwill. The borough is fortunate in having already in existence a lively theatre association and concert society, a flourishing branch of the

Workers Educational Association, and a number of other dramatic and musical organisations. This kind of activity needs adequate accommodation preferably in or near the centre of the town. It is desirable, furthermore, that these bodies should have substantial control of their own facilities and this means that as far as possible they should be able to rent without an excessive strain the premises in which they operate. The rents for brand-new buildings are usually so heavy as to be beyond the means of societies with minority membership such as these. On the other hand they could, corporately, manage to rent older buildings which could be effectively converted to meet their requirements. For cultural and educational activities two kinds of space are needed: an auditorium for dramatic and musical productions, larger meeting rooms for choir practices and orchestral rehearsals and smaller rooms for the purposes of discussion-groups, play-readings, small music groups and the like. For the first the Haymarket Theatre, suitably renovated and extended so as to be joined to the town hall, would provide one useful centre. It might well be complemented by an educational centre, on the pattern of the one at Worthing or of the Associate House at Ashford in Kent, which could make use of the present borough offices, if and when these are vacated, for such activities as require smaller rooms and a congenially mellow atmosphere. As it is intended to build at high density on the eastern side of the town, these two buildings, lying to the south-east of the town centre, would be singularly well-sited.

Central and peripheral amenities

Planning for social provision in the peripheral areas of the town is contingent upon judgements about the effect of the total design of the town upon social activity within it. Until ten or eleven years ago the idea of neighbourhood development at fairly low densities guided the planning of most new towns and housing estates. But by comparison with a typical new town, such as Crawley, Basingstoke is being built to higher densities and for a population in which it is assumed that the average family will possess a car. It is on that basis that the road system has been designed and car parking for 6,000 vehicles is planned for the town centre. The implicitations of these facts are, first, that access to the centre will be easier than in a new town and, secondly, that about 65 per cent of the population, as compared with about 50 per cent in Crawley, will be living within a mile of the centre.

It is difficult to forecast the effect of these differences upon the behaviour of residents, though there is a *prima facie* case for arguing that, by comparison with the new towns, a proportionally higher investment in central amenities than in peripheral ones would be justified. The point clearly requires much more analysis. But, even if that argument were accepted, there are clearly good grounds for making some social provision in the residential areas, though perhaps on a lesser scale than in such towns as Harlow or Crawley.

Of these local amenities, adequate meeting halls in the residential areas are essential for the development of social activities. One of the points which Dr. Nicholson most strongly recommended in his report on new communities in Britain was the timely provision of places in which residents could meet together. The need for such halls is especially acute in the early stages of development when voluntary provision in the form of church halls, for example, is limited by shortage of funds and when the need for encouraging social development is greatest. There can be no question of the desirability of providing initially some kinds of tenants' common room of the kind so successfully used in the estates erected by LCC and Birmingham Corporation. These rooms need not be very elaborate or costly to be effective.

Beyond this, the possibility must be allowed for – perhaps by allocating land for future development adjacent to the tenants' common room – that, as the town grows, there may develop a local demand for some larger facility such as a community centre. Some social activities which are initially based on the tenants' meeting room are likely in due course to find accommodation, for example, in church halls. But there are very often other bodies which are not adequately served either by the tenants' room or by the church halls (both of which are often booked to capacity in new estates) and which are sufficiently well-supported for a case to be made for some more extensive local meeting-place. It is often argued on economic grounds that school buildings ought to be used for such purposes. But special provision is desirable for many activities for which school premises are inconvenient. Activities such as art and handicrafts usually have a lot of equipment and clutter which it is inconvenient to leave in a schoolroom: adult education is better conducted in an atmosphere more conducive to discussion and preferably more comfortable than the average school: while youth activities, too, tend to be better supported if they are conducted away from the school buildings. In addition, it is highly desirable that the people who engage in these various activities should have a say in how the premises in which they meet are conducted: and this element of self-government is much more easily established in a building specially designed for leisure-time pursuits. For the same reason that it is desirable for the users to be associated with the control of the premises, it is better not to provide anything more substantial than a tenants' room until there is a clear and vigorous local demand for it, which can be actively associated with the local authority in providing, running and supporting something as large as a community centre. What the planner must ensure is that sufficient space is left for this kind of future development in the original layout of the scheme.

The location of amenities in the peripheral areas

The second main issue in social planning concerns the location of amenities in residential areas and, in particular, the criteria which should guide the planner in this. One dominant thesis has been that amenities ought to be sited in such a way as to foster a sense of community among the residents. This idea has been incorporated in the neighbourhood unit concept. This concept originated simply as a means of relating amenities systematically to the distribution of population, with some regard to the question of convenience. The size of the unit was originally determined by the fact that one of the main considerations was that small children should not have to cross main roads to get to school and that a population of about 10,000 was required to support a primary school. To this planning theory was then added a social theory which asserted that the neighbourhood plan should also engender a sense of *belonging* among the residents of each residential neighbourhood and that the allocation of amenities should seek to foster community spirit.

It is important to understand the origins of this social theory. It derives from the awareness that developed between the wars, that the early housing estates were not only ill-provided with essential amenities but they that lacked the neighbourliness and the sense of community of the slums. The belief was subsequently generated that the manipulation of the physical environment in the form of the neighbourhood unit might foster these feelings of belonging and neighbourliness.

The chief weakness of this theory lies in its assumption that social characteristics are determined by physical form. The neighbourliness of the slums, however, depended, in my judgment, much less on their physical structure than it did upon the sociological facts that the people who lived in the slums had frequently lived in the same street for one or two generations and under conditions of economic hardship had banded together for mutual help and protection. But it is easily understandable that socially-concerned planners should have supposed that the main causal factor in the development of community feeling was the *physical* environment which it was in their power to modify.

As for the more particular view that a residential unity of, say, 5,000 people will necessarily be more effective in fostering this sense of community than one of 7,000 or 3,000, this is unsubstantiated by any systematic investigation. It is, accordingly, sociological speculation rather than fact; and in the light of the more general argument advanced in the previous paragraph, the presumption is that such minor differences of size have, at the most, only a marginal influence upon social consciousness. Sociologically speaking, none of these figures is better than any other; and if the experience in Hemel Hempstead suggests that a unit of 5,000 people is the best size, then similarly impressionistic evidence, of no more but no less validity, can be adduced from Crawley to suggest that the neighbourhoods there, most of which have between 5,500 and 7,000 residents, have been so successful in generating a sense of local belonging that they are said to have inhibited the development of a sense of identity with the town as a whole. Accordingly, even if there could be shown to be differences in the degree of community feeling as between neighbourhoods of 5,000 or 3,000 or 7,000 people, it can only be an assumption that such differences are caused by the size of the neighbourhoods themselves or by the way in which amenities are disposed within them.

The neighbourhood unit concept, however, is open to criticism on much broader grounds. For, in the first place, it posits the village community as the social ideal at a time when there are good grounds for believing that 'community is becoming a concept which is no longer confined to a particularly locality, or which, indeed, is not primarily to be identified in terms of locality'. And secondly, it is a concept that was developed before the onset of the one-family one-car era and it accordingly loses a good deal of its cogency at a time when people are becoming in every way much more mobile than ever they were.

The location of shops

The application of the doctrine which I am criticising comes out most clearly, at the present stage of Basingstoke's development, in the view advanced by the consultant surveyor that the over-riding criterion in allocating shops should be 'to establish focal points that will foster a sense of "community" within the area served'. I am critical of this view not only on the general grounds advanced above but also because – if one is thinking of the effect of the location of shops on the residents and their welfare, which seems to be the issue – the economic criteria are much more tangible and significant. Clearly, from the point of view of the local authority and trader alike, shops must first of all give an adequate return in relation to the investment costs and the rents. From the consumer's point of view, economy is also vital and what he wants, at best, is economy of purse and time. Shops, in other words, should be both cheap and convenient: and it is an excessively narrow definition of the residents' welfare to focus solely on convenience.

In general, the criterion of cheapness is maximised under conditions of competition and this enjoins a layout in which shops are grouped into centres sufficiently large to permit the presence of at least two shops in all the main trades. This condition would presumably best be met by having all shopping facilities in the town centre, but this would clearly conflict with the other economic criterion of convenience. Ideally what would be required would be an economic calculation of the point at which, trade by trade, cheapness and convenience would break even.

As I understand it, the chief architect-planner envisages, broadly speaking, that shopping groups should be located so as to be within a $\frac{1}{4}$ mile of everyone living in the outer residential areas. I have a good deal of sympathy with the attempt to lay down a quantitative standard of convenience since, without it, this factor is likely to be overborne by other kinds of economic consideration which can be more precisely defined and which thus appear more compelling. But two comments need to be made.

First of all, there is not very much evidence about what people actually regard as a convenient distance. However, I notice that a review of neighbourhood provision in Hemel Hempstead makes the point that people did not wish to have to travel more than a $\frac{1}{4}$ mile on foot to the nearest shops. Be that as it may, the $\frac{1}{4}$-mile formula is a desideratum proposed by the chief architect-planner and not something given in the facts of the situation. Thus, this discipline must be regarded less as a general rule than as a guide, and I notice that the standard has in fact been relaxed in the proposals for South Ham and Kempshott where special circumstances obtain.

The second point is that there is some doubt about how competitive the proposed shopping groups would be. In general, each of the sixteen groups would have an area of 6,000 sq. ft. which it is proposed to divide into one food unit of 2,500 sq. ft., one confectioner, newsagent and tobacconist unit of 15,000 sq. ft., and two other units of 1,000 sq. ft. each. The alternative scale of provision is for 10 groups of 9,000 sq. ft., each serving a slightly larger population and giving a possible allocation of two units of 2,500 and 1,500 sq. ft., plus five others each of 1,000 sq. ft. Clearly, the sixteen groups would be more convenient.

But would commodities like groceries not be dearer? The answer depends upon a judgement about trends in retail trading which I am not competent to assess. The idea of allocating 2,500 sq. ft. as a food unit is to allow for a number of alternative means of provision. The space could either be divided between two multiple grocers or given over to one large food hall. If it were divided between two genuinely competing grocers, then in groceries at least convenience would presumably be matched by cheapness: and the same would apply if the space were allocated for use as a food hall to one firm sufficiently large to be able and ready to pass on economies of scale in keen prices. But in that case there is clearly a danger of affording one large firm a monopoly and of its then exploiting its position, so that the convenience of the ¼-mile principle would be countered by a marginal increase in costs to the consumer.

On economic grounds it might be expected that shopping in a rather larger centre of, say, seven as against four shops would be cheaper to the consumer and more remunerative to the trader. In that case the loss of convenience might be outweighed by a marginal lowering of costs. Clearly, if the tenant's interest is solely in convenience, then there is no question of the desirability of the larger number of shopping groups. But it is clear that the tenant also has an interest in low prices; and, in the absence of any clear method for estimating which of the two alternatives is preferable, the decision is one on which the sociologist *per se* can offer no clear guidance. What he may most usefully contribute to the argument is the informed opinion that the criterion of fostering a sense of community is irrelevant in determining the allocation of shops.

The concentration of amenities

Similar socio-economic criteria ought, in my opinion, to be primary in determining the allocation of all social amenities in residential areas. Clearly what has to be considered first in deciding whether a social amenity, be it a library or a tenants' meeting room, should be provided is what number of people are required to make it worth providing. This criterion then determines the place of the amenity in a hierarchy of areas. As for their location within a residential district, however, there can be little question that the grouping of amenities is more desirable socially than their dispersal. Not only is this more generally convenient but, on the principle that the more shops there are together, the better will be the trade for each, concentration of social facilities like shops, churches, clinics and meeting-halls, affords a greater encouragement to residents using one amenity to make use of the others. This argument applies equally to medical provision, where it is evident that a better standard of service and a more economical use of highly-trained personnel can be achieved through bringing together under one roof a number of general practitioners and ancillary workers like district nurses, health visitors and midwives. Thus, there is every reason to group all local amenities together, though the chief sociological grounds for this policy are that it is more convenient for the residents to arrange them in this way and more likely that they will be fully used. If this grouping also serves to give a social focus to the area, so well and good.

The distribution of different types of housing

In regard to housing the focus of sociological attention in the past has been upon the question whether it is possible, and if so, how to get people of different social classes to live in the same areas. The earlier attempts to do this by building a few managerial houses in predominantly working-class neighbourhoods have clearly failed. This policy again rested upon excessively simple assumptions about how social behaviour might be modified by physical structure and unrealistic ideas about the nature of the British class system. It has to be acknowledged that, socially speaking, the natural thing is for birds of a feather to flock together and that this applies even in working-class housing estates, where a process of transferring from one house to another in the early years of development serves to segregate tenants in precisely this way. No housing policy, however idealistic, can afford to ignore this point.

The design of housing areas, therefore, must accord with the social differences in the community. At this stage, one of the overriding policy considerations is the proportion of houses that should be allocated for renting and for private purchase and where they should be sited. The expectation of a higher-than-average proportion of office-workers coming to the town, the fact that this stratum is steadily growing in size as the economy changes, combined with the knowledge that in Southampton and other towns municipal tenants are tending to buy their own houses, if for no other reason than that in a period of inflation it is more economical to purchase than to rent a house: all these factors suggest that there will be a ready demand in Basingstoke for houses that are offered for sale. Given that in Southampton, for example, over 40 per cent of the houses are owner-occupied, it may be that the allocation of 25 per cent which in Basingstoke it is proposed to develop under private contract, presumably for owner-occupation, is too low.

But since this is so important a matter of general policy, it would perhaps be worthwhile to try to estimate more systematically and empirically than appears so far to have been done what the likely demand for privately-owned houses will be in ten years' time in a town with Basingstoke's population structure.

It is, therefore, inevitable that there should be different types of housing in the town, some of which will be rented and some privately-owned. It is obvious that such differences of tenure, for example, become associated with difference of status. Even though more and more working-class people are now purchasing their own houses, house-ownership is still predominantly a middle-class characteristic. Accordingly the question has to be considered how far it is possible at least to inhibit the development of class animosities by the way in which housing of different kinds is allocated. As I have argued earlier, I am not persuaded that physical planning has more than an indirect effect on social development. Nevertheless it is clear that physical features are frequently used by the people themselves to emphasise existing status differences. In Welwyn, for instance, the railway line effectively segregates the pre-war from the post-war town and serves to accentuate the cleavage between the socially right and the wrong side of the tracks. Excessively sharp points of difference such as that ought wherever possible to be avoided. In Basingstoke, therefore, one might envisage the development in *all* parts of the town of precincts of middle-class, owner-occupied dwellings, each containing perhaps 200–400 houses, distinctive enough in style and layout to attract middle-class residents and yet sharing common social amenities like shops and schools with people of other social strata in the district so that the middle-class areas would not form completely segregated enclaves. An example of what I have in mind is the Park area in Cumbernauld New Town. Too many social benefits must not be expected of such an arrangement however. There is no reason to expect that it alone would induce residents of different classes to participate in common social activities or that it would encourage the middle-class residents to act as leaders in the neighbourhood organisations. Neither could it prevent the assignation of more or less favourable reputations to particular housing areas. All it might do would be to prevent the branding of any one section of the town as better or worse than anywhere else. But that alone would clearly be worth doing.

A further possibility of class segregation must also be briefly considered, namely, that many wealthier incomers may prefer, if at all possible, to live in the villages around the town. In a free community this can be no more avoided than can the acute awareness of invidious status differentials which it will undoubtedly induce among those who might wish but who simply could not afford to do so. From the point of view of the borough as a whole, however, the main danger of such a development is that many people, who might well contribute their leadership and patronage to the well-being of the town, might be ill-disposed to do so since they were living outside its boundaries.

III SOCIAL DEVELOPMENT

In turning finally to consider social development policy, we move from an area in which the statutory authorities are chiefly concerned with the provision of physical amenities to one in which their purpose must rather be to encourage the people themselves to contribute *their* ideas, effort and leadership to the town's well-being. Whereas in physical planning, as I have argued, the chief criterion must be social-economic, in the field of social development, it must be, in that sense, educational. To that extent it clearly calls for a greater sensitivity on the part of the local authorities to local initiative and voluntary enterprise than is either necessary, or perhaps desirable, in designing a housing layout or implementing a drainage scheme.

A social development department?

There are a number of reasons why it might in due course be desirable to constitute within the borough administration a separate department devoted to social development. In the first place, the social side of housing management will inevitably grow in importance as the size of the municipal estate increases. Not only will rent collecting become more onerous, but the number of complaints, both frivolous and serious, the requests for house exchanges and the representations from tenants' associations will all grow apace. It is possible that the housing management staff can be expanded to deal with these new duties: but there are many other related matters with which it would excessively burden a housing department to have to deal and which, in any case, call for a staff more specifically trained in community development. Dr. Nicholson noted in his report that 'most of those who have worked in new communities expressed the view that there should be, from the start, someone with a definite responsibility for social development and, it was often added, a position of sufficient status and independence to ensure that he was consulted on policy'.

The fact that, over the next eight years, an average of thirty families a week and 1,500 a year will be moving into the town indicates statistically the importance of such an appointment. The duties of a social development officer would begin long before the incomers arrived. Mr. L. E. White, who has had long experience of this kind of work at Harlow, has recently made the point that 'if people are to be encouraged to put down roots quickly and play an active part in developing the life of a new community, it is absolutely essential that they should have as much information as possible about the place in which they have come to live'. His initial role would be to act as the authority's information officer. He would also be responsible, through a staff of neighbourhood workers perhaps, for helping the incomers to settle down in the town and to overcome the many social difficulties to which they will inevitably be subject, especially in the early phases. Subsequently he would be concerned to assist and to encourage the growth of all kinds of voluntary social activity. The benefits of this kind of work accrue not only to the incomers who are helped or to the voluntary associations which need initial encouragement and support. They accrue equally to the authority, which, as the chief landlord in the town, gains in goodwill by showing itself from the start to be actively concerned with the welfare of its new residents, and also to industry, which stands to gain from a stable and contented work-force.

One further function might well be assigned to a social development department, which would benefit the work of the local authority as a whole. It might take over the responsibility for intelligence and research. As at least two recent Royal Commissions have made clear, one of the most serious weaknesses in the structure of local government is the absence of effective information and research departments. This gap is particularly noticeable in periods like the present when local authorities have taken on all manner of new responsibilities, notably in the planning field, and when social and economic conditions are changing so rapidly. The absence of a service of this kind tells especially in the early stages of town development when decisions of major importance may often be made with inadequate use of relevant social and economic data. The estimation of the proportion of dwellings to allocate for private ownership seems *prima facie* to be such an instance. It is, furthermore, desirable that planning and architectural decisions should be informed with accurate research about tenant reaction to, say, prefabricated dwellings. Here again, as the RIBA report on architectural practice so clearly showed, social research and the feed-back of information from the site to the drawing-board is most inadequate.

The role of voluntary organisations

On the part of the voluntary associations in the borough, there is already a bubbling of activity which shows that some townspeople are beginning to reflect not only on how the development will affect their property, or the rates, but also on what constructive role they can play in the expansion of the town. The establishment of the citizens advice bureau has been followed by the formation of a social workers' group; the Rotary Club has recently approached the Director of Town Development about how it can contribute and a deputation saw him in 1963 about the development of cultural facilities in the town. These are small beginnings, but they represent useful resources of local goodwill, ability and leadership. At the moment, however, one has the impression that these initiatives are all rather *ad hoc* and that, having no clear idea of what the development will entail, their sponsors are often lacking a sense of direction and any precise idea of what they themselves might contribute to the town's social development.

It is clear that what is urgently needed on the part of the voluntary associations in the town is some coherent idea of what their role should be and some official acknowledgement of the importance of their contribution. One way of achieving these objectives would be the setting up, with the full support of the local authority, of a council of social service. Such an organisation would serve many useful functions. It would draw the voluntary social services together and afford them a forum for discussion and a basis for common action. It would serve to represent these services *vis-à-vis* the local authority in the development of social provision in the town and give them the support, so necessary in a period of very rapid growth, of the expertise and advice of the National Council of Social Service.

A second kind of organisation which would serve the same sort of functions in relation to other kinds of activity is the trust. This applies particularly to sports, education and the arts. It has been very effectively developed in a number of the new towns. In Harlow, for example, trusts have been set up for both art and sport, and in Stevenage, a youth trust was set up a year or two ago, with the support of the Gulbenkian Foundation, to establish a youth centre. Such an organisation has as its purpose to plan for and to co-ordinate efforts to achieve certain kinds of amenity which otherwise would not be provided and for which voluntary support is both necessary and desirable.

The Harlow Sports Trust provides a useful example of what can be done in this way. The trust is registered as a limited company with its main object the provision of facilities for recreation, physical education and other leisure-time pursuits. It includes representatives of the statutory authorities – the county council, urban district council and the development corporation – and two voluntary bodies – the Essex Playing Fields Association and the Sports Centre Supporters Club. It set itself to develop a sports centre at a cost of £100,000 and has raised a substantial proportion of this sum by negotiating grants from the Ministry of Education, the local authorities, national foundations and other interested bodies, by donations from local industry and commerce, and by contributions from the Sports Centre Supporters Club and a penny-a-week contributory scheme. The success of this form of organisation depends upon its being backed by a representative and influential local committee, upon the collaboration between the statutory authorities and the voluntary associations and upon the elaboration of a sound and competently-drafted plan. But in the first instance, from whichever quarter the initiative comes, what is imperative is the full collaboration of the local authorities and the voluntary bodies. There is a need in Basingstoke for trusts of this kind to deal with educational and cultural provision, as well as sport.

The development of community leadership

In all that has been written above in connection with social development, it has been assumed that many more capable local leaders will be forthcoming. But the more the importance of voluntary enterprise is acknowledged, the more exacting are the standards of competence demanded of the voluntary leader. Indeed, if local authorities are to be invited to support voluntary enterprises, they have to be assured that they are soundly conducted. Accordingly one of the most important points which the voluntary associations now need to consider is the competence of their leadership and the efficiency of their organisation. In this connection a local council of social service, if it were established, could do a great deal to improve the quality of voluntary enterprise by offering advice on organisation and by setting up training courses for local leaders, as the London CSS has so successfully done in the GLC estates.

The statutory authorities, for their part, need to be ready to administer the facilities under their control in such a way as to accord, wherever possible, the maximum of responsibility to the local leaders themselves. The relationship between the borough council and the theatre association is in this respect exemplary, for, while the theatre is owned and maintained by the Council, it is managed by the association. This kind of collaboration needs to be fully developed in all

G

manner of communal enterprises. In the administration of tenants' meeting-rooms, for example, as Dr. Nicholson remarks, 'what matters is that neither the planning nor the rules should be so tight as to stifle spontaneity'. For my part, I should be disposed to go further and say that they should positively encourage voluntary enterprise and responsible local leadership by devolving responsibility for the management of tenants' rooms upon the tenants' organisations themselves. Similarly with community centres. Outside Hampshire itself the exemplar here is probably the Moot House at Harlow, which was provided by the development corporation and supported financially by the county education committee who pay the warden's salary and 25 per cent of the running costs. The house is managed, however, by an independent council which appoints the warden and to which he is responsible.

This principle of encouraging local enterprise by according it every support yet leaving it self-governing is of vital importance in social development policy and one which has wide application in a town development scheme. For it is chiefly through administrative arrangements of this kind that the people, who are the chief agents of social development, are likely to make the most effective use of the social amenities which the statutory authorities and voluntary enterprise will provide.

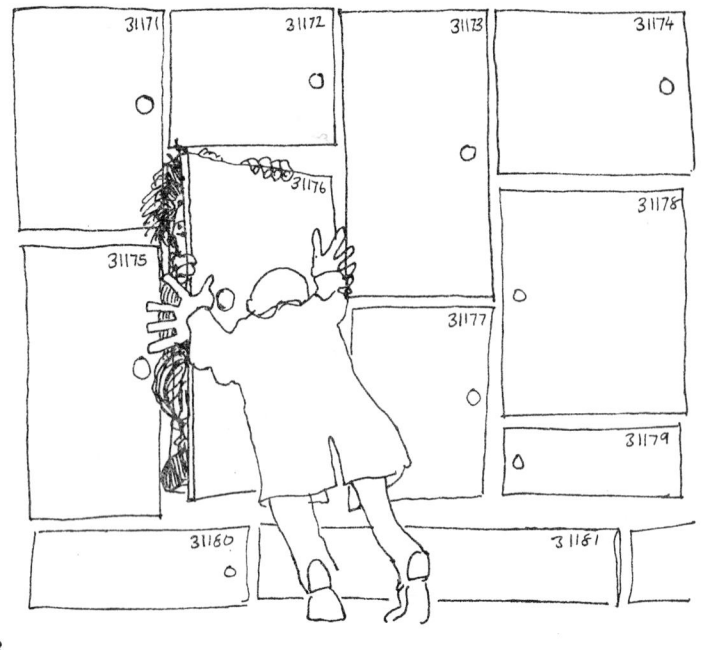

The Social
Context of
Urban Planning

A sociologist discussing urban planning cannot these days count upon
as favourable a reception as he might have had in the early 'fifties.
For the hopes which many planners then placed in sociology have been
shattered by the insignificance of much sociological enquiry claiming
to have a bearing on planning problems and by the inability of academic
sociologists to adapt themselves to the demands of planning practice.
Sociological studies, we are informed, are 'slightly in disfavour among
architects'. We could argue that until recently very few sociologists
were employed in Britain and that the lack of both opportunity and
financial support has inhibited their contribution to planning. Such an
argument, however, would miss the main point that planners and sociologists have very different views of time. The academic sociologist –
and most of us up till now have been employed in academic institutions
– can perhaps afford the luxury of non-commitment. For all his interest
in the idea of scientific prediction, he hesitates to estimate, let alone to
predict the future. The planner, on the other hand, *has* to commit himself *now*, on whatever limited evidence he can scratch together, to anti-
cipations about future circumstances; and I believe that sociologists
will have to come off their scientific hobby-horse and be willing to risk
their necks in making recommendations, using the best available theory
and evidence and even committing themselves to value-judgments,
if they are to contribute in any effective way to the solution of planning
problems.

The planner also needs to rethink his ideas about sociology. Though
the situation is changing, for most planners, in my experience, sociology is represented by Patrick Geddes on the one side and Lewis Mumford on the other. Mumford supports them in the view that sociology
is a general social philosophy, while from Geddes they take the perni-
ciously simple doctrine of 'survey before plan'. The two elements are

related by the naive idea that a survey will establish the facts which will tell the planner exactly how to achieve the social goals which he sets for his town. As a result, sociology comes to be regarded as another kind of market research and the sociologist's contribution to briefing and design is so restricted as to rule out any more theoretically-based analysis.

What this view ignores is that between fact-finding and action lies theory. In briefing a military commander, an intelligence officer will not only report on facts assembled by interrogation and the translation of documents, he will also assess the validity of data he has collected and use them in order to put forward an interpretation or theory about the enemy's dispositions and intentions. The same procedure is also called for in planning. Indeed, it is upon such theorising, as well as upon our knowledge of facts, that our ability to predict depends. Our conviction, for example, that the sun will rise tomorrow over the North Sea and not over the Atlantic depends not only upon the repetition of accurate empirical observations of this particular phenomenon but also upon our having a valid theory of celestial mechanics to explain why the sun never lets us down. In my view, the major intellectual reason for the odd love-hate relationship that planners and sociologists have sustained these past twenty years is that there has been too much simple fact-finding and too little theoretical argument. I turn, therefore, to consider the social context of urban planning with this in mind out of the conviction, so neatly expressed by the psychologist, Kurt Lewin, that 'there is nothing more practical than a good theory'.

Beyond architectural determinism

Now, of course, planners do make use of social theory, though I very much doubt whether they realize that they are doing so. They are inclined to subscribe to a belief in 'architectural determinism'. This theory finds its most enthusiastic expression in comments such as Catherine Bauer's that 'the tenants' entire social life may hang on the smallest whim of the greenest draftsman'. Formally stated, it holds that physical structures determine social behaviour; that the relationship between these two factors is a one-way relationship in which social behaviour is the dependent variable; and that the effect of good physical design on social behaviour will be beneficial and not adverse.

This last point is the clue which helps to explain why planners adopt precisely this form of social theory. For planners, at heart, are social idealists, who believe that their work will help to ameliorate society and even redeem mankind. An architect-planner, however, is technically qualified only in the design of the material environment. What more natural than for him to suppose that the social virtues which his idealism leads him to seek can be promoted by the design of the physical environment which it is uniquely in his power to modify? The trouble with this theory is that it is not a very good one. Like other varieties of popular determinism, it merely saves the layman the bother of observing accurately and thinking clearly. True, bad design can inhibit and good design can make it that much easier for people to do what they wish, or what they are obliged to do. But except in the limiting case, it cannot in my judgment *determine* social activity.

The path along which the sociology of planning needs to go has already been pioneered by industrial sociology. This field has developed, in part, out of the desire to improve industrial productivity, much as planning seeks to improve our social life. But the study of the social organisation of industry has been better financed than research into the social aspects of planning and our understanding of industrial organisation is, therefore, a good deal more advanced. It has gone through three major phases. In the first phase, one can clearly discern the industrial equivalent of architectural determinism. In the classical theory of industrial organisation, embodied in F. W. Taylor's concept of 'scientific management', the worker was regarded as a mere appendage to the machine and his efforts were thought to be determined by purely economic incentives. The analogy with an architectural theory which conceives social well-being as a direct product of good physical design, is, I think, apparent. The second phase, which began in the nineteen-thirties with the work of Elton Mayo, concentrated upon relationships within working groups on the shop floor. The interest in fostering good human relations in industry to which this led in the 'thirties and 'forties antedates by thirty years the planning profession's current concern with citizen participation. Since then, however, our theory has extended still further to take account of the wider structure of social organisation – the pattern of conflict between workers and management, for instance, whose strains have frequently negated management's efforts to improve human relations on the shop-floor. Industrial sociology has thus progressed from a narrow and very pragmatic, to a broader and more theoretically cogent view of industrial organisation. In doing so, it has enabled us to understand, and thus to think and act more rationally about industrial problems. I refer to it here in order to support my contention that a viable sociology of planning equally needs theoretical depth as well as factual content.

A theoretical approach to the sociology of planning

But to the brass tacks of physical planning. The kind of planning problems with which sociologists are asked to deal are usually very specific. Typically, the sociologist in a design team is expected to help prepare schedules of accommodation or to undertake empirical studies of how people use and react to different kinds of housing or layout. Such studies are defined specifically in terms of their utility for physical design; they are highly empirical and they lack theoretical sophistication. Until quite recently the method being used to determine the provision of shops in new developments shared these characteristics. Planning reports of the post-war period contained various statements of the number of shops that could be provided in relation to a given population; and it was in such terms that the problem was still being defined, no more than ten years ago, when Cumbernauld Development Corporation posed the question to three of us at Glasgow University. Our most important contribution to the practical elucidation of the problem was to reformulate it; to place it in a different theoretical context. Instead of thinking simply of the crude ratio of shops to population – and what, anyway, was meant by 'a shop'? – we sought to establish the floor-area that could be used for retail trade and to relate this to population through the intervening variable of annual turnover. By rethinking the problem in this way, we were able to develop a much more viable and rational approach.

Much more could be done along similar lines to make the sociologist's contribution more relevant to problems of physical design. Perhaps the most impressive piece of sociological thinking in this field was the set of projections of housing provision worked out for the abortive Hook New Town which were based upon the theoretical analysis done by Glass and Davidson over ten years before. More work of this kind is possible. For example, all manner of assumptions are presently made in the planning of new towns about the pattern of rents, the size of households, the proportion of dwellings that should be built for sale, et cetera. I suspect that such decisions are presently made either by hunch, by ministerial fiat or by a vague look at what other towns are doing. The disadvantages of such procedures are that they are not fully rational, are not systematically derived from the best available evidence and are often not clearly integrated with other aspects of development policy. These weaknesses could be avoided if we began, for instance, with the theoretical proposition that many factors in housing are related to social class and that this will vary with different economic structures. Then, if one could establish what both an ideal and a probable industrial portfolio would be for a new town, inferences could be made about the occupational-class patterns that these different portfolios would entail and thus about the kind of housing that would broadly match that particular economic structure.

The exploration of such possibilities is best encouraged by the opportunity of applying sociological ideas in the context of urban development schemes; but these opportunities for the sociologist are few and far between. Such procedures are unlikely to produce any final answers that would not need to be revised in the light of subsequent experience: but we no longer expect that of any planning forecast. No: the real value of such methods is that they would make it possible to base certain kinds of planning decision more validly upon evidence and clearly stated assumptions and this would permit a greater control of policy by the regular review of forecasts in the light of actual, on-going experience. At the very least, as the chief architect of a northern new town recently told me, the analysis which I have just proposed would have afforded him a very useful tool in arguing against the limited range of housing which his committee, against his better judgment, had insisted upon.

Social organisation and urban planning

But we can go one step further. We tend to think of planning at the moment as primarily a matter of physical design and land-use. Of recent years we have come to see that physical planning is also closely related to economic planning. The Americans, however, have already jumped beyond this to the view recently spelled out by Dennis O'Harrow of the American Society of Planning Officials, that 'Nowadays we are heading for a troika in which, on an equal basis with land-use planning . . . we shall have social planning and economic planning.'

The point has been pressed home upon the Americans by their experience both at home and in overseas development work. In the United States, the urban renewal projects carried out under the 1954 Housing Act served to highlight problems that most Americans had either not known about or had preferred to ignore. In particular, they brought home the close connection which existed between physical and social blight and subsequently led to the setting up of the Federal Housing and Urban Development Department in 1965 and to the opinion of Robert Weaver, its secretary, that 'today urban renewal must deal with human renewal as well as physical renewal'. Such a conclusion has grown directly out of an urban situation which has involved a scale of physical degradation more serious than we in Britain have faced for fifty years, which has been aggravated by a social schism more explosive than anything that our own class system could have generated, and which is being tackled with a political and legislative apparatus much weaker than that with which we in Britain were tackling the problems of the urban environment in the second half of the nineteenth century.

The significance of social factors has been equally emphasised by the American experience of economic planning in underdeveloped countries. In his book *On the Theory of Social Change*, Everett Hagen posed a question which had puzzled him during the two years he spent as economic adviser to the Burmese Government. Why was it, he asked, that notwithstanding the official desire for economic development, resources were not used more effectively to that end? To answer it, he was obliged to study how different kinds of social structure influenced personality patterns in ways that were favourable or inimical to economic development. Much the same kind of consideration underpins the growing interest in the United States in the social context of planning, the importance of which derives from the observation that the manner of deciding will influence what it is that one *can* decide and is thus bound to influence the results of the decision. In our own context, I believe that the phenomenal growth of sociology in public esteem during the last six or seven years has also been occasioned by an awareness that the retarded pace of our economic development in comparison with other European countries, which became clearly noticeable in the middle 'fifties, was less convincingly explained by reference to the difficulties of post-war reconstruction than to the possibility that our *social* institutions might well be maladapted to the exigencies of rapid economic growth.

In ways such as these, therefore, we have come to appreciate that the pattern of social organisation may have a direct effect upon activity in the sphere of the economy. The point has been more fully developed in that branch of sociology which is known as organisation theory; and the question thus arises, whether this approach has any value for the sociology of urban planning.

I believe that it has. At the micro-level, for example, there is now evidence to show that the attitude of residents to their houses and their satisfaction with them is not affected simply by the objective character of the dwellings but also by whether they are owned or rented and whether the residents have had a hand in building them. On the larger scale, perhaps the most significant work, once again, is developing in America. Jane Jacobs's analysis of the Greenwich Village sidewalk, for example, is an important illustration of the point that physical and social organisation need to be considered together. In her address to the RIBA in 1967, she continued in the same idiom by proposing an explanation of the economic vitality of cities in terms of the relationship between their internal and external economies, a theory which, she clearly believed, would further our understanding of how cities like Pittsburgh could once more be made economically viable. I was particularly impressed with the way in which this organisational approach was being used in the New Town of Columbia in Maryland. The broad social objectives of this development were stated to be to encourage 'the growth in human personality, character and creativity' and to 'increase the options for human development'. We might be inclined to smile a little at this rather grandiose and somewhat utopian expression, of which we in Britain these days are so sceptical. Nevertheless, the working out of these ideas in a report on the planning of social processes *as well as* physical facilities was most impressive.

How little we know – in any systematic way – about the conditions of successful town development in modern Britain! How can the resurgence of the north-east be explained and how far can the experience be applied elsewhere? Or how come that Harlow, of all the Mark I new towns, appears to have had the most successful record of social and cultural development? Though particular individuals undoubtedly played an important role in this development, a distinctive pattern of social and administrative conditions also obtained in Harlow which seems to have been particularly favourable to individual enterprise. At all events, this is the hypothesis that is guiding the pilot investigation which I am presently organising. The factors which I think we shall find to have been particularly relevant are: the sizeable and socially active middle class in Harlow; the significant role played by teachers in activating this middle class; the close relationship between these elements in the social structure and the local administrative agencies; a local council sufficiently in tune with the life of the town and sympathetic towards its voluntary agencies to be willing to engage *their* efforts in its development. Other factors may, in the event, prove to have been more important, but that would in no way invalidate an inquiry from which, I hope, it will be possible to gain some ideas about the conditions of effective social development in growing urban communities.

Planning theory and social indeterminacy
Sociological research can contribute more substantially than hitherto

to the guidance of urban planning. On the one side, it can produce
quantitative estimates of demand relating to physical provision, and I
have suggested that it will do this the more effectively to the degree
that such empirical estimates are rather more firmly rooted in theory.
In the second place, I think we could find out a great deal more about
the specifically social conditions that are conducive to desirable social
results, particularly by the application of a kind of organisation theory
to these problems. However, the question which we now need to
consider is: how far *can* the future be predicted?

One can begin by observing that many architects and planners are
beginning to adapt their practice to the awareness that, under modern
conditions, social change takes place so fast that its direction is difficult
to predict with any degree of precision. John Weeks, for example, has
pointed out that the architect's problem is that his building may be
'sheltering an organisation which has a rate of growth and change . . .
so great that it makes its buildings obsolescent before they decay natur-
ally'. This leads him to the concept of an indeterminate architecture in
which buildings are designed, as far as possible, on a duffel-coat principle in order to accommodate unanticipated changes of social function.
The authors of the South Hampshire Study also noted that planning
was becoming 'less and less a matter of precise propositions committed
to paper and more and more a matter of ideas and policies loosely
assembled, under constant review, within which, every now and then,
some project is seen to be as ready for execution as human judgment
can pronounce'.

These statements indicate a very substantial departure from the idea
that the object of planning is to produce a kind of rational, utopian
blue-print to which future developments will unequivocally conform.
Such an idea is particularly congenial to architects or engineers accustomed to thinking in deterministic terms about the design of buildings
or sewage systems. In its place, we are beginning to get a more sophisticated notion of what planning is about which is at once less utopian
and more realistic in its assumptions about the extent to which we can
anticipate social change. In a particularly interesting article, Otto
Koenigsberger has analysed the reasons for this transition. His starting
point is the dissatisfaction felt in Singapore with British planning of the
period immediately after the war. Here was a plan based upon four
years' intensive and highly professional work; a master-plan 'produced
according to all the rules of the book', but one which had been in-
validated within eight years of its completion by the facts of social
change; by the fact, among others, that the increase of population had

been in the order of 120,000 families per year. Master-planning was clearly not adapted to conditions of rapid social change: and little wonder! For the idea of devising a master-plan was worked out in Britain in the nineteen-thirties and bore the strong imprint of the period of stagnation in which it was conceived. The master-plan was 'fundamentally a static concept of providing for limited and predictable change and ultimately for cities of finite size'. It rested upon the assumptions that social change would be slow, that initiative would come from private parties and that the preservation of an existing beautiful country was a major concern of the planners: assumptions ill-attuned both to the rate of demographic growth in the tropics and to the pace of technological change in our more temperate climes.

I am impressed by the fact that it is precisely the practical men who have come to appreciate the indeterminacy of human affairs. But we also need to consider the possibility that they may have underestimated the potential ability of the social sciences to overcome this indeterminacy by a fuller development of theory and methods, after the manner of the natural sciences. This is a hope that sociologists and architects often share. The zest that many sociologists bring to their professional tasks frequently grows out of the positive belief that social behaviour can in principle (and possibly two or three hundred years' time) be predicted and thus rationally controlled. *Rerum cognoscere causas*, as the LSE has it: to understand the causes of human affairs. Architects, too, are inclined to believe that there must be somewhere – and where better than in a prestige-giving science? – an established theory, a 'scheme for classifying human activities' which would at once resolve the problem of indeterminacy and provide them with a philosophy of design which might be more valid than their own intuitive aesthetic. Some have sought this in Gestalt psychology, some in set theory and finite mathematics; others yet again, have been known to seek their salvation in such odd sources as Malinowski's concept of human needs. Many, in their time, have hoped to find in sociology some such positive approach to design. And so we must inquire whether – as seems often to be supposed – the social sciences can, in principle at least, overcome the social indeterminacy to which our colleagues have begun to accommodate their practice.

The argument has been raging these last ten years in the American social science literature, and I think it is fair to say that the stronger case is being made against, rather than in favour of the presumption. Very briefly stated, the argument has been directed against the idea of planning regarded as an abstract and entirely rational method of establishing the appropriate means to given ends. It has done so, firstly on the grounds that planning is directly affected by the social-political context within which it takes place and that this context does not operate on purely rational principles. The second line of argument points out that man's capacity for problem-solving is very limited, the information at his disposal inadequate to his needs, the variables involved in social affairs indeterminate and so on. It concludes that rationality is 'bounded' and it is accordingly, sceptical of excessive claims on the part of social scientists to be able to predict and control human behaviour.

I find myself in broad sympathy with this conclusion. One certainly does not wish to let premature and entirely *a priori* suppositions stand in the way of the development of a predictive social science; but one is obliged to hazard a guess, as open-mindedly as possible, as to what it is reasonable to expect of the social sciences, given the nature of human behaviour. Though there are clearly regularities in social conduct, which it is the function of sociology to elicit and explain, and which give grounds for hoping that prediction is possible, I think that the circumstances affecting their validation and use are so different from those operative in the physical sciences that I do not share the hope that sociology might become a predictive science in any comparable sense. My reasons for this are the following. First of all, it is not possible to establish *by direct experiment* the conditions under which social regularities obtain. We must fall back, accordingly, upon sleight of hand like the *ceteribus paribus* clause in economics or upon what we might call 'mental experiments' which, though important and useful, establish proof a good deal less convincingly than can be done in the truly experimental sciences. Secondly, the particular future circumstances in which a sociological generalisation may be applied are likely to differ in highly relevant respects, whose significance may not at first be appreciated, from the conditions originally postulated for it to be valid. Thirdly, the fact that human beings can know what social scientists find out about their behaviour makes it possible for them in some degree to control that behaviour and even to succeed in invalidating the propositions thus made. In other words, I consider that human life, unlike natural phenomena, is for most purposes best regarded dialectically, as a constant interaction between an objective and a subjectively-defined reality.

I conclude, therefore, that social behaviour, though in many respects susceptible of limited prediction, does not permit the sociologist to claim for his predictions the same degree of assurance that the physical scientist is commonly believed to have in his. It is inevitably indeterminate and it is more reasonable to accept this fact, as Weeks and Koenigsberger have done, and to revise our ideas about the nature of planning accordingly, than to continue to work upon the assumption that sociology, for example, can by some uncanny magic really make it possible for the planner to produce absolute blue-prints for our future well-being.

Planning in a new context of theory

To argue like this is, in effect, to propose a changed view of the place of the person in the planning process. As the American planner John Friedmann has noted, the blue-print model of planning raises the problem of how to get the subjects of planning to act in accordance with the blue-print; people are viewed simply as objects which have to be made to conform to the plan. A planning theory which acknowledges social indeterminacy, on the other hand, while in no way denying the importance of determining in advance what it is possible to anticipate, also requires the planner to allow for and to adapt sympathetically to new contingencies that arise unpremeditatedly within a society; among which perhaps the most important are the social initiatives which develop within a community through civic action.

This view is consistent with the dialectical conception of human existence. Consider a marriage, for example. Clearly, a good deal can be predicted about its course. We can estimate things like the probable number of children that will be born, the likelihood of the death of one partner or the other in any particular year, and so on. Actuarial practice depends upon a knowledge of such probabilities. But it would be impossible to predict what specific quality of human relationships, what flowering or deadening of the human personality might follow from the development of that family; or what potential it might release among its members which otherwise would have lain dormant or taken, perhaps, a very different course. Such characteristics, though not predictable, are nevertheless viable and objective social facts which need to be comprehended in any valid sociology and which, in my view, must also be incorporated into any theory of social planning.

A brief review of one current issue in planning theory will point up what I mean. We appear to be accepting the view that only a town with a population of, perhaps, more than a quarter of a million can provide adequate social and cultural facilities. The recent plan of the Paris region, for example, states that only new urban centres, serving between 300,000 and a million people can sustain a cultural centre, a theatre or a concert hall. Of course, a minimum clientele is needed for a theatre to be economically viable. Planners, however, ignore the fact that theatres have recently been built and flourish in places like Guildford with a population of only 50,000 or Chichester with 20,000: and probably the reason they do so is that, professionally, they think only of such gross physical characteristics and have no occasion to consider the significance of the social resources that have made such developments possible. It is true that the major contributions to the physical development of towns are made by statutory and commercial agencies which provide, on the one hand, what is statutorily obligatory and, on the other hand, what is profitable. But many other desirable contributions are made by civic initiative and it is these initiatives, which are usually impossible to anticipate very far in advance, which are the concern of that kind of planning which has to do with social development.

Social development in this sense is likely to become more and more important in the urban planning of the future. A society which is increasingly based upon an advanced technology inevitably requires greater centralisation of power: and this would seem likely to decrease the degree of autonomous activity at the level of the local community. This, however, has not so far been the case. For an advanced technology also demands a higher level of education and a greater degree of responsibility among the labour force. This is usually thought of in economic terms, as an aspect of man-power planning. But it also has a major effect on the community since it is now well-established that initiative and social participation in community activities increase with social status and education. It is the expansion of this more articulate stratum in our own society, at a time when the growing centralisation of political and economic power puts the ordinary citizen increasingly at the mercy of the vast oligarchies of our age, which accounts for the very rapid growth of consumer societies and civic groups which, since the war, has given the lie to the view that voluntary civic action would be made redundant by the establishment of the Welfare State.

Now it is pretty clear that the planning profession is in something of a quandary in adapting to such groups. On the one hand, planners often hark back to the view, more characteristic of the early utopian than of the present-day, bureaucratised phase of planning, that 'planning is for people' and that they should be actively associated with the development of their own communities. This doctrine now finds pragmatic support in the belief that the participation of the citizen will make planning more effective and planners less despised. Against this, there is the hard fact that planning is now part of the machinery of government and is thus influenced by the administrator's characteristic assumption that the ideal situation is one in which the public authorities provide such satisfactory services that the citizens are content to allow the officials to conduct their affairs without interference, an ideal in which the best testimony to administrative efficiency would be a completely passive citizenry.

This kind of assumption was appropriate enough in the early nineteenth century when our present system of local government was set up in response to the urban problems thrown up by the early phases of capitalist entrepreneurship. It had three major characteristics. First of all, it was chiefly responsible for providing tangible things like streets and sewers and lighting and for the maintenance of law and order. Secondly, there was a great disparity of status between the members and officials of local councils and those for whom municipal services were provided. Thirdly, the latter were effectively a *lumpenproletariat* uneducated, not yet enfranchised and subject to long hours of routine, manual employment. In such circumstances, it is not surprising that government should have been conceived as the provision by a strong executive of services needed by a largely – indeed, ideally – passive and deferential population.

These assumptions, however appropriate they might have been in the heyday of the steam-technology of the last century, are less well adapted to the conditions set up by the scientific-technological revolution in which we now find ourselves. Government, for one thing, is now responsible for services like education, which not only affect the personal life of the citizen more directly than did the provision of the streets but which require for their efficient prosecution his witting concurrence, if not active collaboration. Such services are likely to become increasingly important in the future. Furthermore, the status disparity between the citizen and those who control the public services is now diminishing, if it is not in many places completely eliminated; while the citizen himself is less disposed to accept the passive and acquiescent role to which, on earlier assumptions, he was relegated. Our governmental system is operating in the twentieth century with a set of attitudes towards the public which largely derive from the nineteenth. The tension to which this leads is felt throughout the system; but I think it is felt particularly in the planning departments partly because of their very rapid rise in importance since 1947, partly because planning, which, in any event, sounds suspect and even dictatorial, so tangibly affects people's private affairs, and partly because, being the most important recent addition to our governmental structure and manned by a profession still rather unsure about its credentials, they are more than usually sensitive to their public relations.

Citizen participation

Structural tensions such as these make themselves felt in the public arena in the forms of issues – in this case, citizen participation. Interest in this idea grows chiefly out of the planners' concern with their public image. Citizen participation, therefore, has been placed in the rather limited context of professional self-interest rather than in the broader framework of social theory. Consequently, it is typically regarded as a technique for getting people to comply with planning proposals more easily. In Max Lock's recent exposition, for instance, it was put forward as if it were a kind of wonder soap-powder, containing magic new ingredients, which would guarantee, as he himself put it, 'surprisingly quick results'.

Such an approach is bound to be inadequate, as a review of the many papers on this theme will show, which the *Town Planning Institute Journal* has published these last few years. The major defects derive from the fact that the idea has been taken over as a kind of gimmick from American practice, with far too little consideration of the more general issues involved and virtually no study of the relevant American literature.

The main theoretical consideration which is at issue here is that American planning administration, like the American political system as a whole, is fractured and diffuse while our own is centralized and highly co-ordinated. In Britain, the local planning departments are agents of national policy, embodied in statutes and regulations, which impose upon them obligations backed by the authority of the State. In the United States, on the other hand, planning is done by innumerable differently-constituted and variously-financed public and semi-public agencies. Effective local action thus depends upon the negotiation of a consensus among such agencies in support of initiatives that must originate within the local community. As a result, some kind of participation by civic groups is expected in the American setting and, indeed, demanded if the local political system is ever to achieve anything whereas, in Britain, this kind of civic involvement is neither expected nor encouraged, nor is it quite so requisite for the operation of the system.

A study of the relevant American literature throws light upon the qualifications which must be borne in mind in any assessment of the

American practice of citizen participation. In the first place, the term 'citizen', with its very favourable connotation, can be used to cover the participation not only of indigenous community associations or leagues of women voters but also of the economically powerful and usually conservative organisations of big business, which often dominate American city politics. Citizen participation, in short, may be no more than a cover for the exploitation of economic self-interest. In such circumstances, the citizen may get merely the form, rather than the reality of participation. One commentator, for instance, has noted that 'too frequently it consists of a limited discussion of only a portion of the planning commission's completed work by a group carefully selected by a mayor or chamber of commerce official'. Furthermore, there is a good deal of evidence that American planners, despite all the rather glib talk about its value, try to defend their activities against what they regard as unjustified civic participation. Thus, the comparative effectiveness of urban redevelopment in Newark, New Jersey, was due to the housing authority's being able to win for itself such a large measure of political independence that it had no need to conciliate grass-roots organisations. In Chicago, important though civic initiative was in setting city planning in motion, its subsequent role was limited to forming a favourable public opinion rather than to determining actual planning proposals. Even in Philadelphia, where Ed Bacon's interest in citizen participation is well known, the original idea of developing plans by a process of group discussion proved disappointing, while the Planning Commission's enthusiasm for involving citizens actively in the planning process was tempered by the planners' claims to professional autonomy. This kind of evidence surely supports us in the view that professional prerogatives and professional judgments need to be defended against the excesses of citizen enthusiasm.

The tenants' association in Glasgow was challenging the whole fabric of political authority, by *demanding* that the corporation provide a bowling green in its part of the Pollok estate and by threatening that its members would withhold paying their rates if the demand were not met on the grounds that 'we've been paying taxes for same for years'. But how well-defended our officials are, compared with American officials, who operate so much more directly under public observation and who are dogged by the populist assumption of American government, which takes it for granted that the ordinary citizen has a right – indeed, a sacred duty – to interfere in the day-to-day conduct of public affairs. The British teacher, for example, can afford to snub the parent-teacher association; the American cannot. By the same token, the

American planner always has to be looking over his shoulder to see who will be shooting at him next, requiring a public examination of his conduct. His British counterpart, on the contrary, is protected from scrutiny by the aristocratic-derivative conventions of our structure of government and, in particular, by the formal separation of politics and administration. That surely means that the British planner can negotiate with citizen groups from strength and that, one might have hoped, would have made the relationship so much more viable.

The official, however, almost invariably thinks that such groups are merely hostile and critical, unless of course, they can be turned to use and support through citizen-participation techniques. It is often argued that they are ill-informed and merely negative; but this cannot be said of the more recent manifestations of civic action in relation to planning. A more viable argument is that they are merely (note the perjorative tone) a sectional interest. Clearly, this may well be the case. The proposals being advanced by the Barnsbury Association in Islington to restore the early Victorian terraces around Gibson Square as a middle class, professional enclave could easily be regarded with hostility by their old-established working-class neighbours, living in dank and decrepit dwellings, who might see in the *demolition* of this older property their only hope of getting a new council house. The function of a council is to make decisions about the balance of public interest involved in cases of this kind. That having been agreed, however, we must go on to say that not all decisions of every council are – beyond question and public inquiry – in the public interest. Nor is every sectional interest necessarily opposed to some notion of public well-being which is vouchsafed to the local council. On the contrary, civic art collections and adult education classes, for example, are catering in fact for only a small minority of towns' citizens, but they are thought none the less to be a proper object of public subsidy. What is more to the point, the vitality of a town depends on the activity of sectional interests, like local chambers of commerce or drama societies, and very often desirable social facilities, such as family planning clinics and marriage guidance centres, are provided only because a group of citizens get together to make sure that such needs are met. Citizen participation, accordingly, is not only an adjunct to planning in a purely technical sense. Viewed in a broader theoretical context, it can be seen to have an important and positive part to play in the democratic social development of urban areas which a comprehensive planning policy would surely seek to foster.

Social planning an integral part of urban development
The degree of acceptance which such a proposition is likely to secure
will depend upon how planning is conceived. One approach considers
the purpose of planning as being to 'rationalise the activities on which it
is imposed: to make subject to calculation what was previously left to
chance, to organise what was previously left unorganised, to replace
spontaneous adjustment with deliberate control'. Such a view of urban
planning is plausible enough, to the extent that planning has grown
out of the desire to control by rational means the adverse consequences
of uncontrolled development. The danger is that it is too rational by
far: for proponents of this approach are inclined to suppose that spontaneous, unorganised, chance activities *need* to be brought under
rational control. They thus allow a concern for order and regularity to
blind them to the significance of such activities in a vigorous social life.
Jane Jacobs's attack upon the injection of 'cataclysmic money' into massive and deadening redevelopment projects and her delicate analysis of
the Greenwich Village sidewalk, Christopher Alexander's critique of a
rigidly hierarchical approach to urban design: these indicate an appreciation of the value of spontaneity and variety in urban organisation
which is complemented, in the drabber atmosphere of British planning,
by the greater flexibility which the Planning Advisory Group's report
enjoined and which one might hope to see spread over into our thinking about the specifically social aspects of urban development.

The kind of social planning which is here envisaged is very different
from the technical, objective process of trying to predict schedules of
accommodation for physical design with which this account began.
It is something like an educational process, in which the community
planner enters into a direct and active engagement with a developing
social structure. Karl Mannheim spoke, in this sense, of engaging in 'an
experimental process of common endeavour'. In a rather more specific
context, Roland Warren, the professor of community theory at
Brandeis University, has described the object of social planning as the
mobilisation of effort in order to improve situations which are per-
ceived as social problems. This kind of work is essentially a process of
social interaction, in which the planner is not primarily concerned with
physical provision as such, but rather seeks to encourage social initiatives within the community so that its members may contribute more
fully to its development. The relevant techniques are being fashioned,
particularly in the United States, in the community-action programmes
that are being developed under the Economic Opportunity Act in the
slum areas of great cities like Pittsburgh, and right at the other extreme,

in the social design of new towns like Columbia to which I have already referred. Here in Britain, it is being worked out in the practice of several community development officers and neighbourhood workers up and down the country, while my own approach has been to make use of adult educational techniques to make it possible, for example, for voluntary associations in Basingstoke, Maidstone and Southampton, and now in South Buckinghamshire and Farnham to work out reports on particular local problems, which give a stimulus and a direction to subsequent social initiatives.

This rather experimental work in applied sociology is calling in question the static conception of social planning which we have again inherited from the nineteen-thirties. The problems with which conventional planning is presently concerned are the problems of the inter-war council housing estates: how to provide social facilities other than houses; how to relate them to the growth of population; how to foster a sense of belonging in new housing areas and how to encourage leadership within the community. The publication of the Housing Advisory Committee's report on the needs of new communities shows that the problems of social provision have at last received official acknowledgment, even though practice still lags far behind our understanding of the needs. But however important physical provision may be, we may well find in twenty years' time, that we have recognised it just at the time when we should have been thinking equally seriously about the neglected fourth item of concern that grew out of the nineteen-thirties – how to encourage an indigenous leadership. Except that now, in the nineteen-sixties – and even more so in the 'seventies and 'eighties if my analysis is valid – there is not going to be a lack of civic leadership so much as a lack of intelligent collaboration with it on the part of our public authorities and a lack of the ability to devise organisational patterns to match new opportunities. This is shown by the fact that so few projects have matured to take advantage of the £4 per head of population which, since 1963, it has been possible to levy for social development projects in the new towns. For the option has fallen foul of the inability of the development corporations, local authorities and voluntary associations to find formulae for co-operation and finance. A good town is not only a well designed town. It is also one in which problems of social organisation of this kind can be resolved, and civic initiatives liberated. That is the function which this new concept of social planning has to fulfil.

'A government (wrote John Stuart Mill) is to be judged by its action upon men, and by its action upon things; by what it makes of the citizens, and what it does with them.' Written with idealistic prescience, six years before the Reform Act of 1867, Mill is speaking directly to our condition. For the new scientific-cum-technological civilisation into which we are rapidly moving demands a population which is increasingly inclined to organise in order to promote civic initiatives. This is occurring at a time when the growing centralisation of control, which is equally a product of technological development, makes such active citizenship even more needful and desirable for the well-being of our democracy. In developing countries, such as India, as well as in technologically advanced societies like the United States, the importance of associating human resources with physical and economic development is being accepted and a practice of doing so worked out. This is the issue which will face us more and more as our urban areas develop into the future. The indeterminacy which we have come to acknowledge, and the greater flexibility in planning which this acknowledgment has engendered, are favourable conditions for its solution. The practical development of these ideas, however, is presently inhibited by our regarding planning as a matter of land-use and economics. Planning in Britain has also got to be thought of as a process for encouraging and making it possible for the *human* resources of a town or a region to contribute more effectively to its social development. This point of view is not easily assimilated in a society which, in so many ways, has shown itself unwilling or unable to foster the potential of its people.

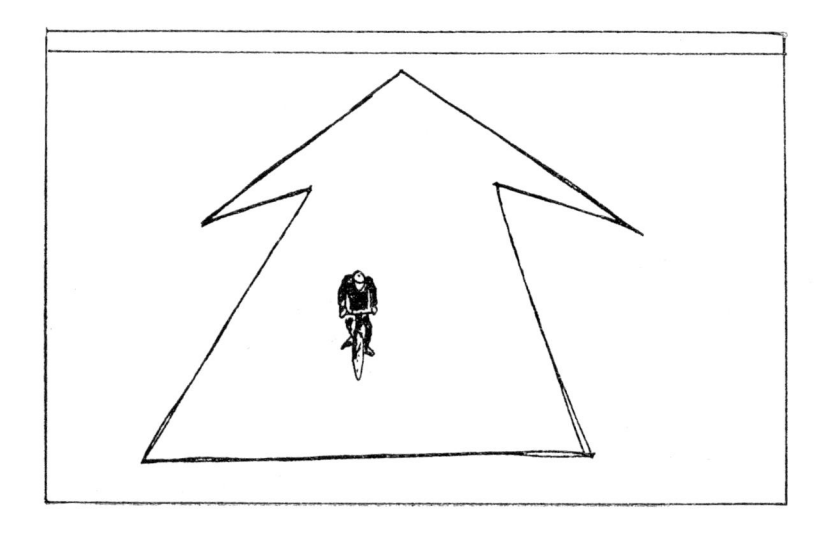

1 **'Social Theory in Architectural Design'**
Architectural Association Journal, vol. 81, no. 898 (January 1966).
Translated version under the title 'Warnung vor Weltverbesserern'
appeared in *Neues Forum*, XIV Jahr, Hefte 165 and 166 (September
and October 1967)

2 **'Social Theory and the Total Environment'**
Northern Architect, vol. 1, no. 2 (June 1967). Slightly shorter version
published as 'Social Theory and the Planners', *New Society*, no. 229
(16th February 1967)

3 **'Community Power and Voluntary Initiative'**
Prepared for the annual conference of the Standing Conference of
Councils of Social Service 1964, *Social Service Quarterly*, vol. 38,
no. 3 (Winter 1964)

4 **'Social Change and Town Development'**
Prepared for the annual conference of the Town and Country
Planning Association 1963, *Town Planning Review*, vol. 36, no. 3
(January 1966)

5 **'The Idea of Social Planning'**
Prepared for the 1967 Congress of the Royal Society of Health
under the title 'Social Planning in the City Region', *Journal of the
Town Planning Institute*, vol. 54, no. 5 (May 1968)

6 **'The Social Aspects of a Town Development Scheme'**
Prepared for the Basingstoke Town Development Joint Committee, published in H. Wentworth Eldredge *ed.*, *Exploding Metropolis*,
vol. 2 (New York, Doubleday/Anchor 1967)

7 'The Social Context of Urban Planning'
Prepared for the first Alcan Universities Conference, Newcastle,
1967. Forthcoming publication in *Urban Affairs Quarterly* (March
1969) and *Kölner Zeitschrift für Soziologie und Sozialpsychologie*